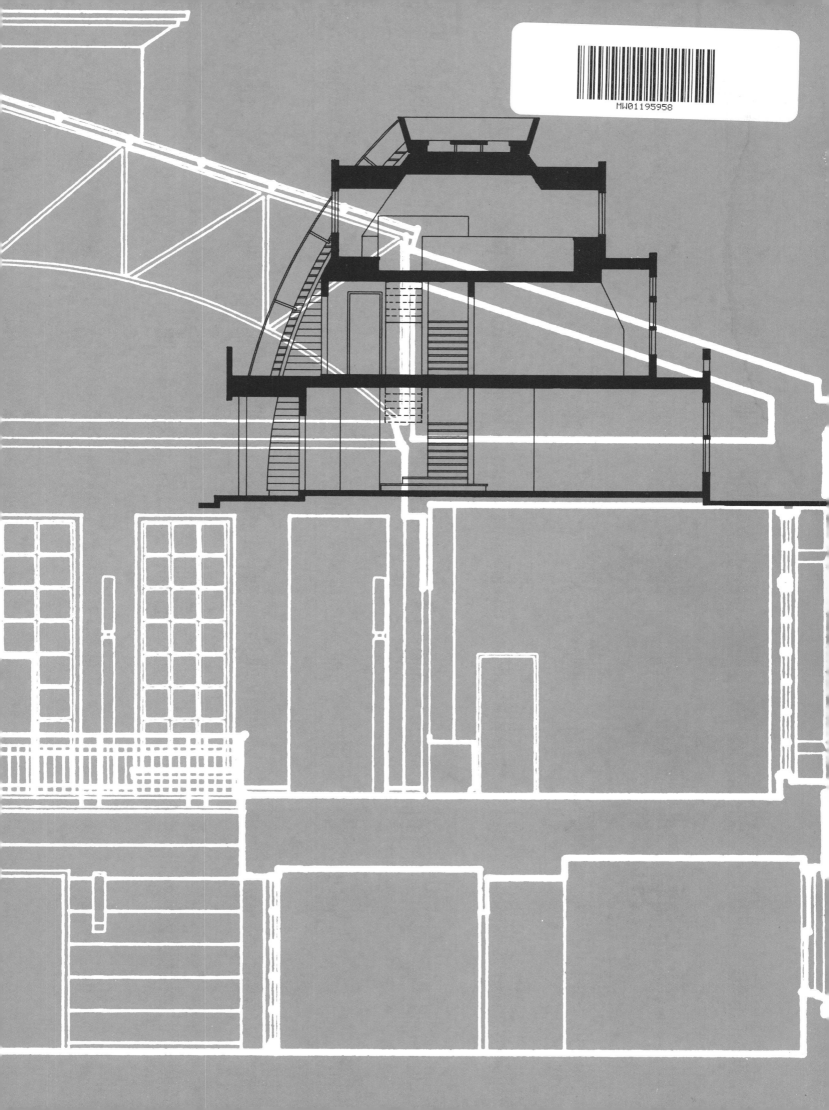

GRAHAM GUND
ARCHITECTS

The American Institute of Architects Press

Washington, D.C.

With a Foreword by Vincent Scully

GRAHAM GUND
ARCHITECTS

First published in the
United States of America in 1993 by
The American Institute of Architects Press
1735 New York Avenue, N.W.
Washington, D.C. 20006-5292
800/365-2724

Library of Congress Cataloging-in-Publication Data
Graham Gund Architects / American Institute of Architects Press ;
    [foreword by Vincent Scully ; introduction by Graham Gund].
        p. cm.
    Includes bibliographical references and index.
    ISBN 1-55835-093-4
    1. Graham Gund Architects (Firm)--Catalogs. 2. Architecture,
Modern--20th century--United States--Catalogs. I. Graham Gund
Architects (Firm)   II. American Institute of Architects Press,
NA737.G717A4 1993
720'.92'2--dc20   93-33663
                                                      CIP

Design and type composition:
Group C Inc
NEW HAVEN
(BC, RF, DK, JR, CS, FS)

Text for this book was set in ITC New Baskerville using
small caps and old style figures.

Printed by D. W. Friesen, Altona, Manitoba, through
Four Colour Imports Ltd., Louisville, Kentucky

Front cover: Fernbank Museum of Natural History
Photograph © Jonathan Hillyer

Back cover: Cohen Residence
Photograph © Warren Jagger

Back flap: 75 State Street
Photograph © Steve Rosenthal

Title page: Patterson Residence
Photograph © Steve Rosenthal

Contents page: Boston Ballet
Photograph © Steve Rosenthal

This book, like our buildings, is the product of efforts made by many sets of eyes and many pairs of hands. The energetic, enthusiastic, and talented staff who have been my faithful collaborators and extended family over the years are deserving of my deepest expression of gratitude. Specific recognition is due to my partner Peter Madsen and the outstanding group of associates who lead our projects: George Coon, James Cullion, John Prokos, Alec Holser, Laura Sanden Cabo, Youngmin Jahan, Elizabeth Redman Bramhall, Jonilla Dorsten, and Mary Horst.

In addition, special thanks are owed to Jonilla Dorsten whose wonderful powers of insight and expression served to inspire and inform the introduction; to Betsie Redman Bramhall for her months of hard work in developing the manuscript; to Katie Barrows for her tireless efforts in gathering and deploying the countless visual ingredients; to Ping Mo and his crew of draftspeople for the handsome drawings they produced; and to Peter Madsen for providing a guiding hand to all.

Thanks also to Steve Rosenthal for his cooperation in rounding up reams of photographic images; to Brad Collins, Catherine Sandler, and Juliette Robbins of Group C for a marvelous job of design and production; to John Ray Hoke, Jr., FAIA and Janet Rumbarger of the AIA Press for their vision and commitment to the project; and especially to Vincent Scully, whom I have long respected and admired as a person and a distinguished scholar, and who has honored me and all those with whom I work by contributing to this monograph.

G.G.

CONTENTS

Projects

8

Waterville Valley Town Square

Graham Gund has to be valued as a convinced preservationist, and that role, accompanied by related strategies it suggests, is probably the most important that an architect can play at this moment in urban history. American cities were torn apart a generation ago by the automobile and the utopian horrors of International Style planning—soon followed by the disintegration of community in part brought about by that process—and the most serious architects and planners of the past thirty years have been trying to put them back together again. Their efforts have been assisted and in good measure motivated and enforced by the only mass popular movement to have materially affected the course of architecture since World War II, the movement toward historic preservation. At present that powerful political force is being directed with increasing boldness by the National Trust for Historic Preservation, of which Graham Gund is a hardworking trustee. Its concerns are now reaching out from the preservation of individual buildings to that of center city neighborhoods and their inhabitants, and to its councils Gund brings his special experience as an architect and an urban developer.

As an urbanist, Gund's finest achievement so far has probably been his "historic rehabilitation" of the six beautiful judicial buildings composing Bulfinch Square and his creative adaptation of them as an office development and public park. In that adaptation he left them alone as much as possible, and his own offices and others now benefit from the wonderful courtroom spaces they occupy. More important, though, is the general rehabilitation of the neighborhood, which the public park has helped bring about.

It is unusually significant here, I think, that the original courthouse was designed by Charles Bulfinch, because the flavor of Bulfinch's high, thin, geometrically activated brick facade is present in one way or another in all of Gund's work. That relationship may have begun in part because Gund's earliest projects, like the Institute of Contemporary Art and the School-House on Monument

Square, were of a kind wherein the interiors of old buildings were entirely scooped out and redesigned in a very free and open manner and the exterior walls were left as they were. This immediately causes them to look like thin shells, in part divorced from the interior spaces, which could be seen all open and brightly lighted behind them. This must have helped suggest the very free treatment of facades that has characterized so much of Gund's later work, such as One Faneuil Hall Square, the Inn at Harvard, and the Boston Ballet. Bulfinch is consistently brought to mind by these buildings, as are older types, such as Queen Anne, which stand farther back in Boston's past and its European antecedents. The rather bouncy freedom with which Gund scatters rectangular, square, diamond-shaped, round-headed, and circular windows across these facades has been criticized as "toy-like" and indeed seems to drive some of our more dour critics mad with rage. It all looks too easy to them and too frivolous to be taken seriously as architecture. There are questions of propriety here that are not so easy to decide as the modern movement once thought they were. To be sure, the Ballet Building does dance; one is not so sure what the Harvard Inn does–though, like the Williston Library at Mt. Holyoke College, it conceals a convincingly robust Renaissance courtyard behind it.

At the same time a good many of Gund's details, though not usually his plans (which in larger buildings are sometimes disconcertingly *echt* GSD), derive obviously enough from Robert Venturi, sometimes from Venturi filtered through the younger Robert Stern. In the old days of the High Modern Hero Architect, that would have been enough to put them out of court. But is originality of much importance in architecture, where the question should always be the place as a whole, not the individual building? Architects in the periods when cities were built best all used each others' details more or less; that was one way everything held together. Still, Gund consistently refuses to be

"correct." He abstracts and deforms his traditional details in ways that stricter revivalists now regard as cartoonish. So his suburban houses and related buildings of moderate scale, such as the Horizon Admissions Building at Connecticut College, all with their Shingle Style planning reminiscent in particular of Bruce Price, are not by any means correctly Shingle Style in detail, and all emphasize, with their big thinly mullioned windows and, often, latticed surfaces—their extreme, touching thinness, like lanterns blooming with the lighted space inside.

Beyond such questions, though, there are some buildings by Gund about whose quality there cannot be much disagreement. Northeastern's boathouse on the Charles River is surely one of them, absolutely right and appropriate in its place. Golden Eagle Lodge is another: a vast hotel built very simply but echoing and reechoing and commenting lovingly on all the profiles and deep slopes of the mountain behind it, while down below, by the lake, the Waterville Valley Town Square is reflected in the still waters and by its own long mountain ridge in the distance.

The Village Commons on South Hadley is harder to assess, but it should be compared with Andres Duany's and Elizabeth Plater-Zyberk's commons in Mashpee, where a shopping center is being turned into a town. In South Hadley the attempt is to re-create a new shopping center for a town which, like so many others, has seen the heart of its community destroyed by suburban malls. Here the visual effects experienced by walking through the meticulously arranged and detailed buildings of the group, all white and gleaming on their steep slope, are lush and sometimes very moving. It is the old American dream of Eden regained. We can hope it will one day be extended to the devastated communities of Center City as well. Theoretically at least, Gund's architecture would like to do exactly that.

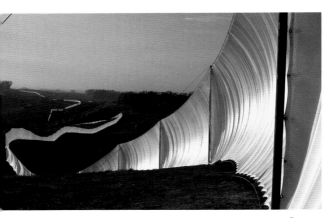

figure 1

figure 2

Each of us sees the world through slightly different lenses. Mine, it seems, frames a vision that, since childhood, has been shaped by a passion for art and by a fascination with the artistic notions of our time. Through architecture I have found a means to explore these artistic ideas in a direct and concrete way, using visual abstraction and spatial relationships to influence perception and to evoke feeling.

The act of making architecture is very much an artistic exercise. Finding one's way through a building design or an urban plan is not altogether different from finding one's way across a canvas. As architects and planners, our language is space and form, and our canvas is earth, sky, and city. Design to us is a process of exploration and discovery in which our relationship to the environment is constantly revisited, reinvented, and redefined.

This process of exploration for me has been informed by the thinking of such contemporary artists as Kenneth Noland, Morris Louis, Ellsworth Kelly, Frank Stella, and Christo. Noland, Louis, and Kelly explore the illusion of three dimensionality through expansiveness, color, shaped canvases, the extension of images off the canvas, and an alternating rhythm of focus and diffusion, creating a total environment in which the viewer participates. Stella and Christo also explore literal three dimensionality in pursuit of similar ends. Just as their explorations begin to erode the edge between art and architecture, blurring the line between the space of the work and the space of the viewer, so ours at Graham Gund Architects communicate ideas both through the relationship of the building to its context and through the engagement of the person in the experience of the place created.

Christo's *Running Fence* (1976; figure 1) is an installation that harmonizes with, and casts new light on, its context. It brings humanity into the landscape and defines a way for the eye to move through a boundless natural canvas. The Golden Eagle Lodge is for me an exploration of similar artistic ideas. It is a reflection and an enhancement of its natural context. Its

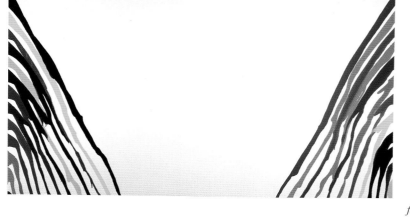

figure 3

meandering form echoes the rise and fall of the White Mountain landscape. The edges of its form are indiscernible from the forms of its natural context. The Patterson residence on Fisher's Island is an organic extension of its natural context as well. It rises like a landform on the horizon or like a ship with billowing sails at sea. It also speaks to its architectural context by referencing the Island's tradition of great roofed houses densely populated with varied dormers. These projects explore the harmonious coexistence of built and natural forms as a means of interweaving figure and ground.

While the Golden Eagle Lodge expresses harmonious life on the land, the Waterville Valley Town Center uses simple forms and repetitive fenestration to express the power of the built order in the natural world. It provides a highly ordered center to an untamed landscape, much as the single yellow rectangle in the *Sun in the Foliage* (1964; figure 2) by Hans Hofmann provides an expansive and strong focus to a richly textured surface.

The ideas expressed in Louis's art are particularly relevant to many of our urban architecture projects. By extending the color fields off the edge of the canvas, Louis explores how the ambiguous relationship between figure and field begins to erode the edge of the framed rectangle. Likewise, Church Court, in historic Back Bay, obscures the edge between the space of place and the space of the city. The rhythm of the bays and banding that defines the character of the historic streetfront is reinterpreted and woven through the new construction. The edge between the space of place and the space of the city is obscured. At Mount Holyoke, the Gothic vocabulary of the original library, that of its various additions, and that of the campus context finds new life in our Science and Technology addition. The proportions of the openings, the texture of the surface, the horizontal banding, and the rhythm of bays all serve to unify old and new into a single composition. The new is born of an understanding of the layers of history and specific qualities of nature that have combined to create the place.

Noland and Kelly both use shaped canvases and broad areas of color to explore ambiguities between exaggerated spatial perspective, perceived depth, and two dimensionality. Their works erode the edge between the space of the viewer and the work of art. The Shapleigh summer residence explores similar ideas through the play of diagonal and frontal relationships within the courtyard. The sequence through the Institute of Contemporary Art similarly juxtaposes diagonal movement against an orthogonal defining envelope. In both of these spaces this juxtaposition engages the person into the experience of the space.

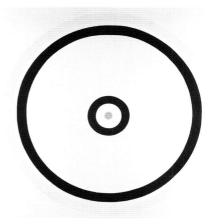

figure 4

I am fascinated by the choices that Morris Louis makes in the placement of the color fields and the juxtaposition of the colors as he addresses his canvases. In *Delta Lambda* (1961; figure 3), he explores the idea of the center and the light found there. At Mount Holyoke, a light-filled court was literally carved out of layer after layer of accrued building. The space provides the tranquil ground to the soaring Gothic mass of building. At the Fernbank Museum of Natural History, the center is shifted to the edge between the building and the landscape, the edge between the man-made and the natural. Here, center mediates between the two worlds, one monumental and highly ordered, the other natural and seemingly chaotic.

Plimoth Plantation and the Nesbeda residence are examples of center seen in a different light. They draw upon lessons learned from works like Kenneth Noland's *Inner Way* (1961; figure 4), where the focus alternates between center and edge and the enclosing rectangle is an arbitrary delineation. The boundary of the canvas is seemingly limitless, as is the vastness of the landscape into which these buildings are set. The center and the edge, the inside and the outside, represent here not opposites but two ways of seeing a continuous field.

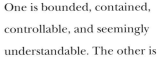

figure 5

figure 6

One is bounded, contained, controllable, and seemingly understandable. The other is beyond knowing. One is the garden, the other the wilderness. In the garden, we understand the movement of the sun, the changing of the seasons, and the passage of time. Outside of the garden we are a part of the wilderness.

In *Beth Heh* (1958; figure 5) and in many of Morris Louis's Veil paintings, the color seemingly ascends the canvas as if by divine proclamation, recognizing that the sides are very different from the top and bottom of the rectangle. Depth is achieved through an application of layers of thinned color, which creates a sense of enclosure modulated by the underlying structure of the canvas. In the octagonal reading room at Mount Holyoke, similar ideas of verticality are explored. The trusswork seems to grow up from the ground. The eye moves from bottom to top and enclosure is achieved in an organic way like the space created by the canopy of a tree. These ideas are explored on a grander scale within Westminster Theater, where the rich patterning of walls and ceiling creates a continuous enclosure almost half spherical in feeling.

Kenneth Noland's *Via Blues* (1967; figure 6) explores movement across and through the canvas by the layering of horizontal stripes of color. The juxtaposition of different colors creates the illusion of depth. This exploration has many architectural parallels. At the Davis residence, the plan is layered from the city to the sea with the support space relating to the former and the ceremonial space relating to the latter. The house is also layered vertically from open to enclosed. The Carroll Center for the Blind is an exploration of the layering of spaces from light to dark and the layering of textures, all intended to speak to the senses. The metaphorical garden stair hall at the School-House is an exploration of the layers of space within the picture plane. It is a concrete expression of more abstract ideas explored by Frank Stella in works like *Sat Bhai* (1978; figure 7).

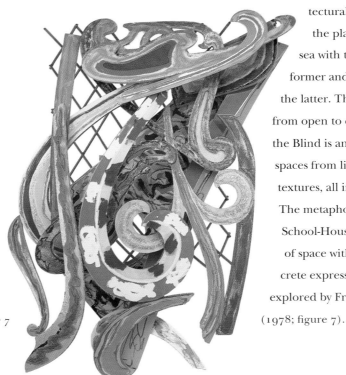

figure 7

The art of Nancy Graves and Jess enables us to see our "everyday world" in a new way. Their work seems to mediate between the accidental and the chosen, between life and art. In *Trace* (1979–80; figure 8), Nancy Graves evokes the translucent properties of trees suggesting light-touched foliage and luminous blue sky. The lobby of the School-House combines abstracted elements to create the feeling of a garden. The form of and the elements within the atrium at Monument Square allude to the water, the earth, and their celestial ceiling. The sky is even filled with winged creatures.

Jess in *The Virtue of Incertitude Perplexing the Vice of Definition* (1972; figure 9), incorporates objects from daily life into the fictive world within his work. This shift in context empowers the objects with new communicative potential. In the Deutsch residence, a garden trellis is applied over the exterior of the upper floors, evoking the feeling of a garden gazebo. At South Hadley, giant leaves pattern one of the Village Common buildings, reinterpreting the ivy-covered buildings of its academic neighbor. The cast stone patterning at the Lincoln School alludes to Stick Style framing, evoking a romantic architecture and implying an inclusive, humanistic approach to education. Rich patterns in marble, gold leaf, and glass combine in the facades of 75 State Street to form a unified whole. The simple shapes of the graphic elements convey one message individually and another in unity.

Our role is as caretaker of urban space and natural form. We see the city as a repository of our communal artifacts and the landscape as a connection to our communal birth. What we build must naturally address the past as it speaks to the future. We are caretakers and tailors, preserving and repairing the fabric of the place we inhabit.

figure 8

figure 9

The former Perkins School looks much as it has for years in this established urban neighborhood, with only new windows and balconies signaling its conversion to residential use. Inside, the building's public space, once a simple elementary school corridor and dingy fire stair, now a novel and dramatic work of environmental art, provides a bold and contemporary contrast to the historic exterior.

The new lobby is a metaphorical garden filled with colorful references to sunlight, nature, and weather. A glazed vestibule wall at the entrance is expressed as a glass-enclosed trellis, while freestanding elements and fixed walls within the lobby form a setting for abstracted forms—trees, flowers, rocks, rays, waterfalls, clouds, sunsets and stalactites. This lobby landscape is linked by a sinuous chrome vine handrail and granite steps, which make entry and circulation through the building's core an unconventional and engaging experience.

Twenty-one apartments occupy former classroom, attic, and basement spaces. Units are configured to take advantage of the oversized schoolhouse windows, which provide abundant light and views. The sitting areas of each classroom unit, and the entire basement floor are elevated three steps to establish a more comfortable residential relationship to the high windowsills.

The attic space, with its complicated trussed framing system, contains six units: three flats and three duplexes. Reverse dormers provide ample natural light to each unit and retain the cornice line of the building in accordance with preservation guidelines established by the neighborhood.

THE SCHOOL-HOUSE

BOSTON, MASSACHUSETTS

The chrome handrail turns into a vine as it descends past the tree forms. The vertical red element, a bold punch of color, is the fruit of the vines.

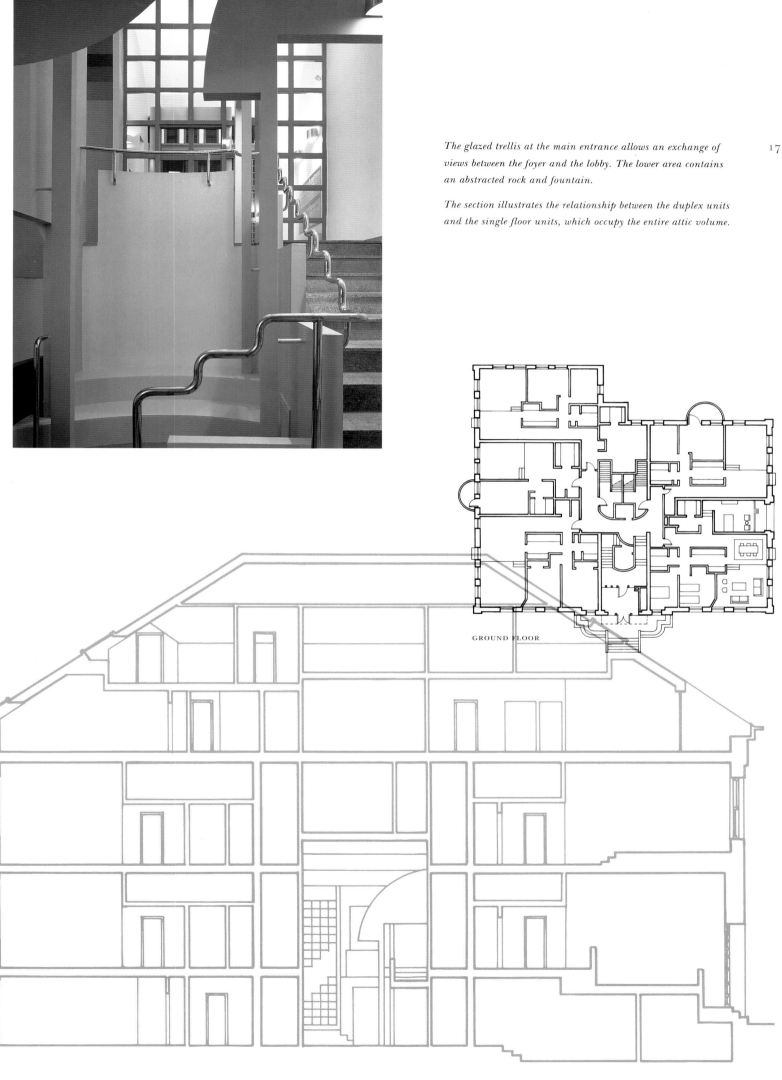

The glazed trellis at the main entrance allows an exchange of views between the foyer and the lobby. The lower area contains an abstracted rock and fountain.

The section illustrates the relationship between the duplex units and the single floor units, which occupy the entire attic volume.

GROUND FLOOR

The glass-enclosed reverse dormer creates a large third-floor deck space and provides views of the surrounding urban neighborhood.

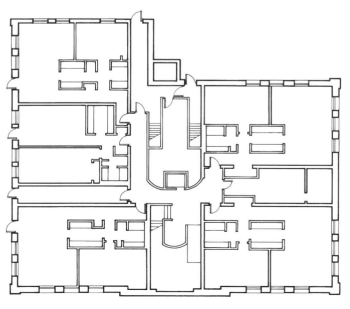

FIRST FLOOR

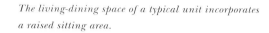

The living-dining space of a typical unit incorporates a raised sitting area.

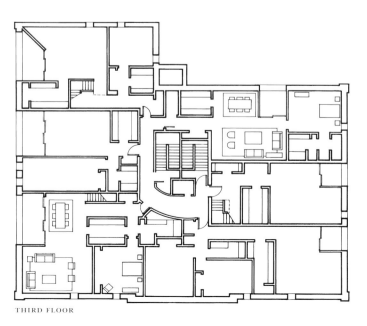

THIRD FLOOR

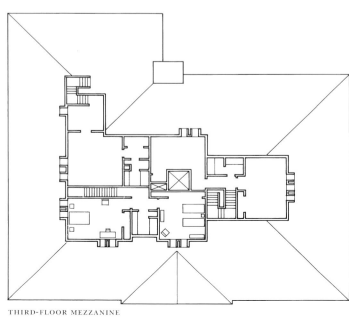

THIRD-FLOOR MEZZANINE

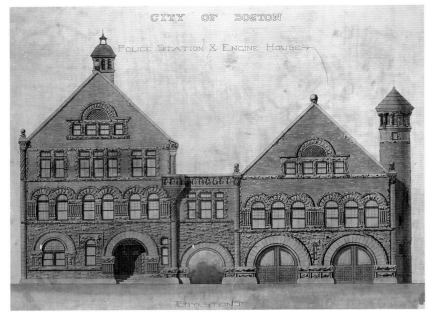

Conceptually, the Institute of Contemporary Art exploits contrasts between old and new, historic and modern, as a way of expressing the institute's contemporary place in historic Boston and in the world of art. The gallery is located in the heart of the city's arts district in a landmark building that was a former police station. This important example of late nineteenth century Romanesque architecture, with its weighty Richardsonian wrapper, serves as a perfect foil for the ethereal contemporary treatment within.

Inside, walls that once enclosed jail cells are removed to reclaim a large open volume. Two new structural elements replace a web of existing columns and rise alongside an existing chimney stack like trees within a landscape of stairs and gallery spaces. The void implied by the columns is rotated within the space to separate it from the side walls, allowing the stair volume within to wind at split levels through its interior.

Art and architecture become one and engage the viewer in the experience of the space—itself an artistic creation—which is viewed at different angles and levels from the stair, heightening a sense of movement and delight within an everchanging visual landscape.

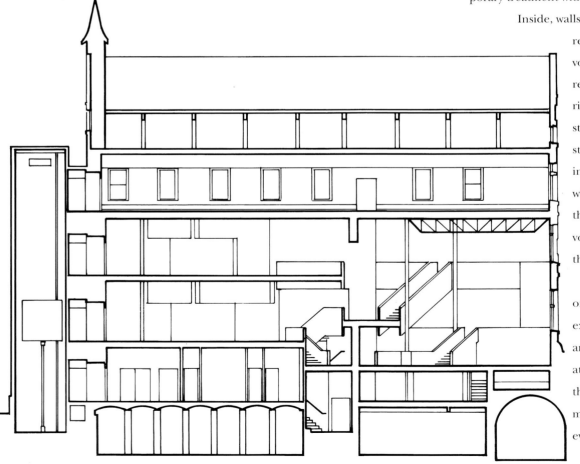

INSTITUTE OF CONTEMPORARY ART

BOSTON, MASSACHUSETTS

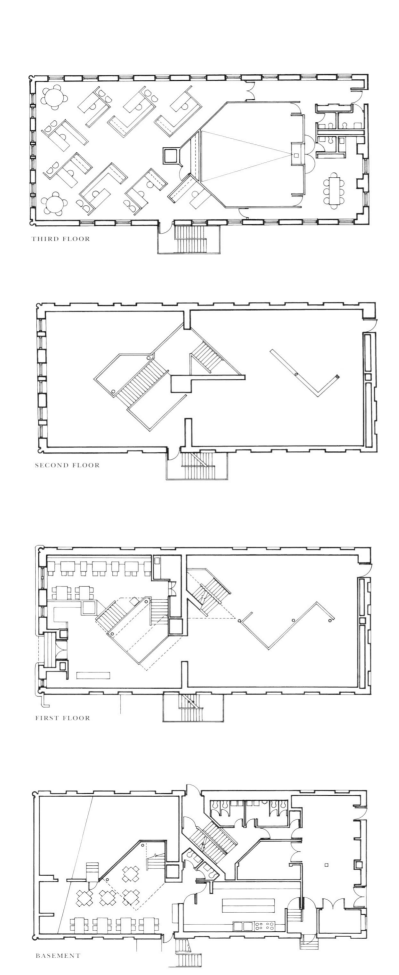

THIRD FLOOR

SECOND FLOOR

FIRST FLOOR

BASEMENT

From a single point of entry, connections are made to the institute's two prominent program spaces. Stairs lead down a level to the restaurant, while a narrow bridge crossing the restaurant's airspace leads to the first floor gallery and to other stairs.

The diagonal grid of the new columns floats the spaces in the center of the building and opens up views between floors.

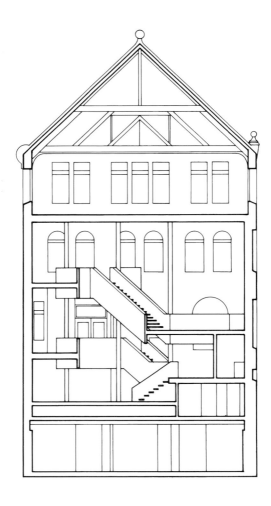

Diagonal relationships of plan in the Institute of Contemporary Art create a complexity and drama that are revealed as the viewer moves through the space.

A brilliantly illuminated central atrium carved from the interior of a former riding stable is the physical and emotional focal point for this training facility for newly blind adults.

An existing skylight is transformed into a new light well, which opens into the atrium and serves as a point of orientation. A new trellis surrounds the light well, giving it special prominence for the sighted. High ceilings and a variety of textures within the space provide auditory clues, which help to orient individuals and enhance their understanding and appreciation of the space.

Light from a second existing well, an enlarged rectangle above a second floor lounge, passes through new interior windows (actually salvaged cabinet doors from the stable's old tack room) to a balcony and into the central atrium beyond.

The modulation of light, texture, and spatial volumes—often perceptible to the blind—plays an important role in the design of the facility. Throughout the building, layers of space (small and large, low and high, open and closed, hushed and busy) work with variations in finishes (carpet against tile, wood against stone) to create a richness of texture and to heighten the sensory experience for the blind and sighted alike.

CARROLL CENTER FOR THE BLIND

NEWTON, MASSACHUSETTS

The staircase in the atrium of the Carroll Center, which brings light all the way to the ground floor, is marked by an oversized newel post on which an inspirational quotation from the center's founder is inscribed in braille.

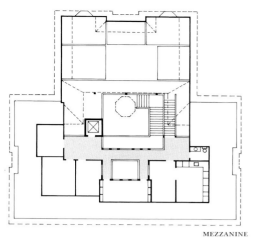

MEZZANINE

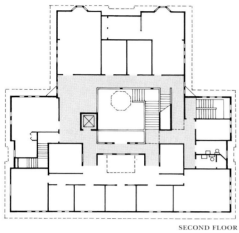

SECOND FLOOR

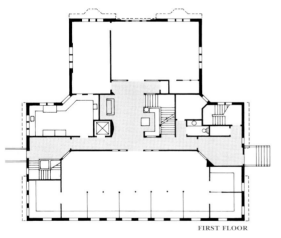

FIRST FLOOR

The former horse stalls on the first floor have been reclaimed with minimal intervention and are being used as teaching space.

SHAPLEIGH SUMMER RESIDENCE

SOUTH DARTMOUTH, MASSACHUSETTS

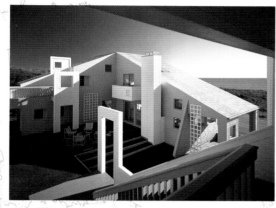

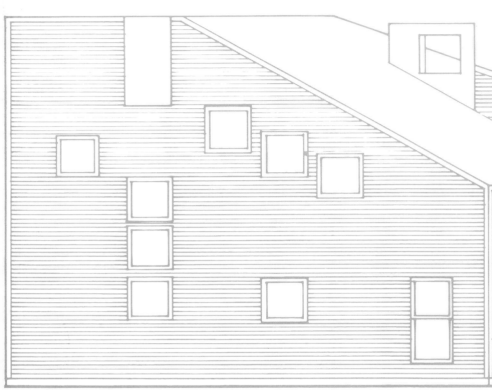

This house is a coastal retreat for an extended family and speaks to the needs of the group and its individuals, balancing opportunities for participation and privacy, while taking full advantage of the spectacular view and the light.

The house is organized as a cluster of three wings around an outdoor courtyard space. The master wing is a winterized structure, which includes dining, living, and kitchen spaces for large group entertaining, a bedroom for the parents, laundry, and internal circulation. A separate wing designed for warm weather use contains a smaller kitchen, dining and living space, four bedrooms for adult children, three loft hideaways for grandchildren, and an external circulation system. A third wing, housing a garage and storage structure, completes the grouping.

A prevailing onshore wind was the functional genesis of the courtyard. The architectural activity in this protected space—a busy family of stairs, chimneys, trellises, walkways—reflects the human activity of the space. Rooms of the summer wing open directly onto this space, screened from view by the walls supporting the second level open walkway.

The outer perimeter of the house is sheathed in weathered shingles to relate to the neighboring houses. The courtyard is constructed of clapboards and painted in eight colors to enhance its animation.

Circulation occurs through and around the courtyard on two levels and joins an interior stair to the third level roof deck for a dramatic 360-degree view of the surrounding peninsula and ocean.

The three main buildings of the Shapleigh Residence are open at the corners, allowing entry and views of Buzzards Bay beyond.

The views of the architectural activity within the courtyard change constantly
as one moves around the building on the second-floor walkway.

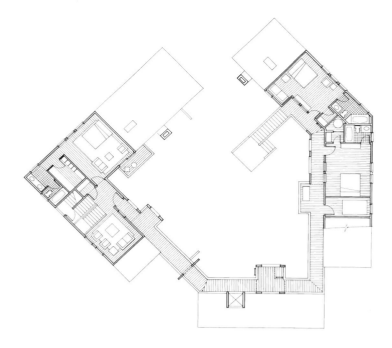

SECOND FLOOR

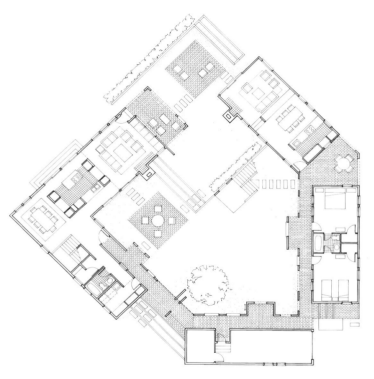

FIRST FLOOR

*The living room in the guesthouse treats views of the
architecture like artwork.*

*The main house living room is open to the porch and the view beyond.
Light from skylights filters through colored baffles in the living room.*

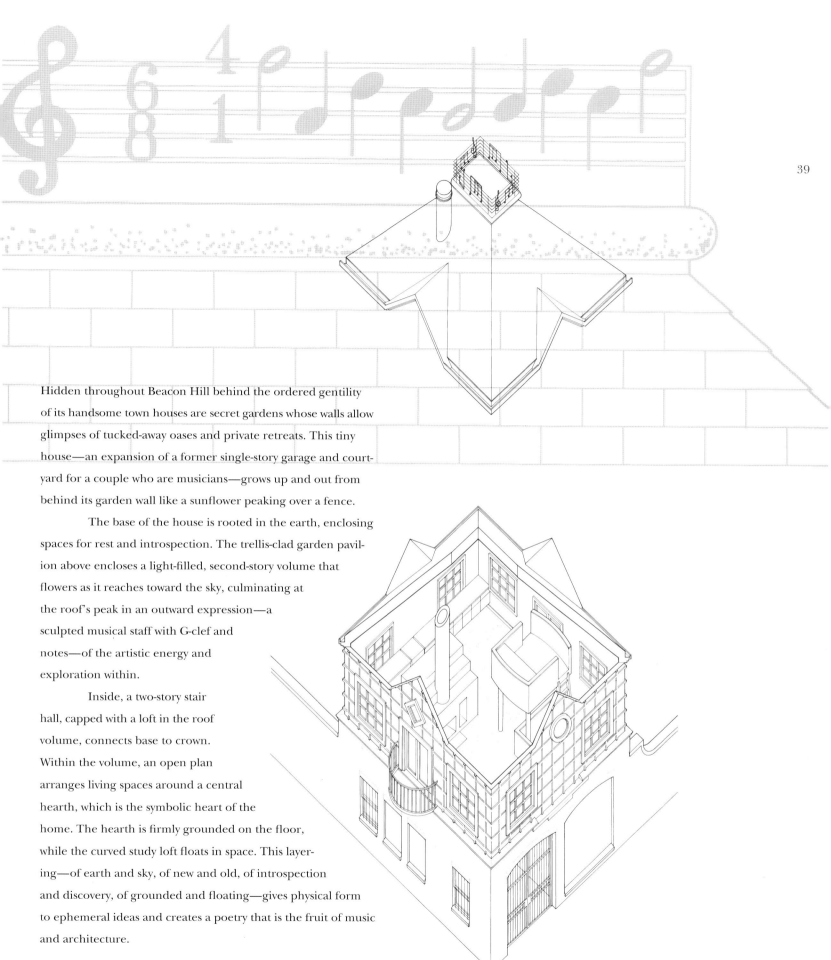

Hidden throughout Beacon Hill behind the ordered gentility of its handsome town houses are secret gardens whose walls allow glimpses of tucked-away oases and private retreats. This tiny house—an expansion of a former single-story garage and court-yard for a couple who are musicians—grows up and out from behind its garden wall like a sunflower peaking over a fence.

The base of the house is rooted in the earth, enclosing spaces for rest and introspection. The trellis-clad garden pavil-ion above encloses a light-filled, second-story volume that flowers as it reaches toward the sky, culminating at the roof's peak in an outward expression—a sculpted musical staff with G-clef and notes—of the artistic energy and exploration within.

Inside, a two-story stair hall, capped with a loft in the roof volume, connects base to crown. Within the volume, an open plan arranges living spaces around a central hearth, which is the symbolic heart of the home. The hearth is firmly grounded on the floor, while the curved study loft floats in space. This layer-ing—of earth and sky, of new and old, of introspection and discovery, of grounded and floating—gives physical form to ephemeral ideas and creates a poetry that is the fruit of music and architecture.

DEUTSCH RESIDENCE

BOSTON, MASSACHUSETTS

40

FIRST FLOOR

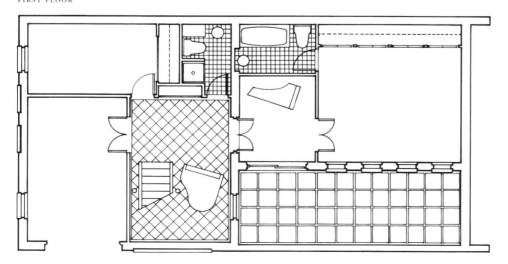

SECOND FLOOR

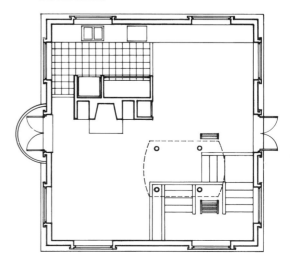

LOFT

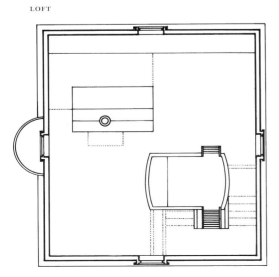

The activities of the Deutsch house are focused in one volume. A visual tension is created between the fireplace, rising out of the floor, and the study, hovering in the air on light columns. The plans show the rebuilt first floor and new second and loft levels.

CHURCH COURT

BOSTON, MASSACHUSETTS

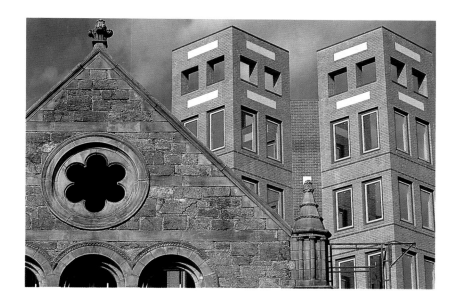

The festive wrapper created a heightened sense of anticipation prior to the unveiling of the new riverfront facade.

45

The traditional brick of the neighborhood's late nineteenth century row houses, with ornamental detailing of limestone and brownstone, is interpreted freely in the new facades of Church Court.

46

The layering of new upon old adds excitement and richness to the urban fabric of Boston and, through a collage of varied architectural forms and changing building uses, speaks to the growth of the city over time. Church Court finds its place within this collage, incorporating the burned-out ruin of a landmark 1891 church into a new 43-unit condominium building.

Three town houses, including a seven-level tower unit, are created from the church remains. A new seven-story addition wraps around the stone ruins,

creating a cloisterlike courtyard garden where the church sanctuary once stood and continuing the architectural scale and dignity of the historic Back Bay neighborhood.

New openings cut in the old exterior masonry walls make it clear that the building is no longer a church. The triple arched former entry doors are left permanently open on their original hinges, and their openings are glazed, revealing the new landscaped space within.

The broadly bowed facade that faces the river resembles a billowing sail. Its grand scale, viewed appropriately from the Charles River, contrasts sharply with the smaller scale of the courtyard. Here, through the use of bold strokes of color and pattern, the two-dimensional surface takes on the apparent depth of nineteenth century construction.

The courtyard plan pulls the building's units away from the busy urban street, allowing for the creation of garden apartments at ground level. As a mediating space, the courtyard protects the architectural integrity of the church walls by creating a respectful distance between old and new facades. It brings light and views to all units and relates the building to its neighbors—by carrying the neighborhood's front garden theme from the street to the apron of the interior units, and by turning the architectural rhythm of the street, with its bowed fronts and projecting bays, into the courtyard.

The walls of the new building, seen through the old church doorways, extend the Back Bay town house vocabulary and become part of the neighborhood fabric.

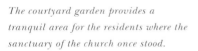

From the south town house living room there is a view of a sculpted bronze angel, commissioned for the project.

The courtyard garden provides a tranquil area for the residents where the sanctuary of the church once stood.

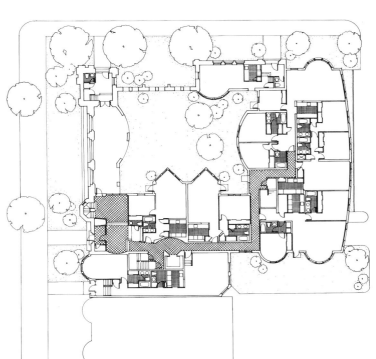

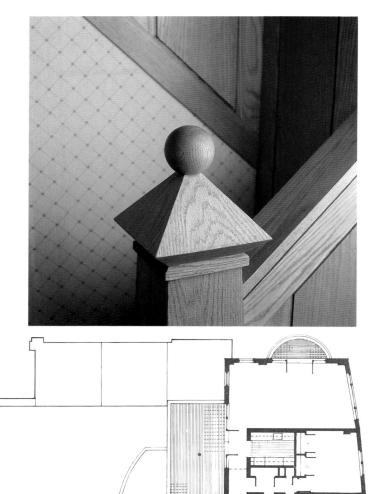

The living room of the tower is in the former belfry, seven levels above the street.

The lobby in the addition abstracts ecclesiastical motifs from the church as a way of linking old and new parts of the building.

The first floor of this modest summer house on the southern coast of Massachusetts was conceived as a living porch, part indoor and part outdoor, defined by a broad, sheltering roof. Here "house" is reduced to its essence of roof and columns; its plan and section speak about a layering, from land to sea and earth to sky, of spaces and forms. A sheared entry facade presents a wall to the street, where a solid service core marks passage through the house. Beyond this core, a meandering interior wall, reminiscent of the coastline, defines two octagonal forms that float within the volume and distinguishes indoor living space from outdoor living space as the house moves toward the water's edge.

      The second floor, by contrast, is a cozy place, where bedrooms are nestled protectively under the volume of the roof. A family of playful dormers pokes up from the sloped roof to frame views of the ocean. In the children's room, a triangular skylight is stacked above a round one, creating views from both top and bottom bunks. An open stair hall ascends beyond the second floor to a roof deck offering a panoramic view of the surrounding peninsula.

DAVIS RESIDENCE

SOUTH DARTMOUTH, MASSACHUSETTS

FIRST FLOOR

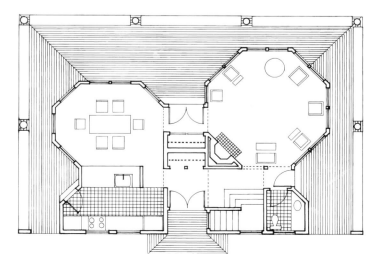

SECOND FLOOR

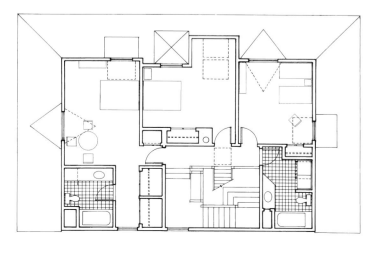

The octagonal first floor living spaces float within the
rectangular frame of the porch which wraps around three
sides of the Davis house. The two-story stair hall leads
to a roof deck.

BULFINCH SQUARE

CAMBRIDGE, MASSACHUSETTS

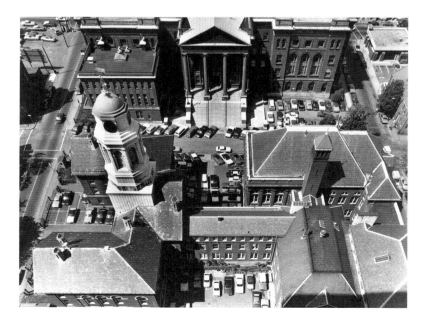

Before and after views show the creation of the courtyard at the heart of Bulfinch Square.

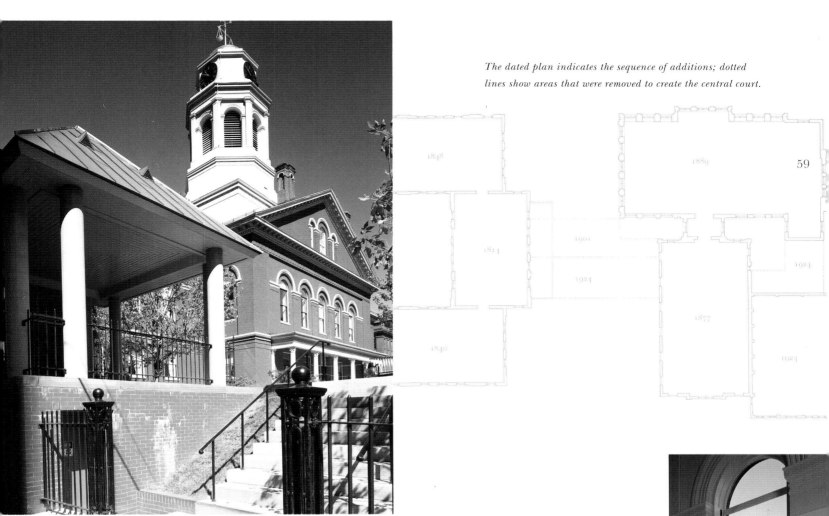

59

Bulfinch Square is the antique rehabilitation of six historic courthouse buildings into an intimately scaled commercial office development and public park. The project not only restores the architectural integrity of the individual buildings, but also mends a decaying urban fabric by reintroducing the restored complex into the larger neighborhood as a vital element.

Originally designed in 1814 by the noted American architect Charles Bulfinch, the courthouse was significantly enlarged over the years until it became a complex of buildings. Two twentieth century additions, in 1901 and 1924, obscured the original Bulfinch facade and destroyed the architectural integrity of the nineteenth century buildings.

Following the construction in 1974 of a modern high-rise judicial facility across the street, the historic courthouse complex was abandoned and the buildings, which then sat vacant for ten years, were slated for demolition. Through our efforts, those of the preservation community, and others, the complex was saved for reuse.

The process of reconstruction actually began with the demolition of three "link" structures (including the 1901 and 1924 additions which had obscured the original Bulfinch facade) and with the reclamation of their footprints as open space. Conceived as a courtyard, this "new" space is harnessed as the organizing element for Bulfinch Square, unifying the group into a comfortable and coherent whole while allowing each structure to retain its own distinct presence. Enclosed by two existing buildings and two new garden structures, this space, with the restored Bulfinch building as its focal piece, acts as a gathering place for workers and visitors.

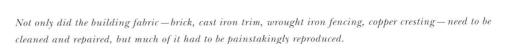

Not only did the building fabric—brick, cast iron trim, wrought iron fencing, copper cresting—need to be cleaned and repaired, but much of it had to be painstakingly reproduced.

*One meticulously restored two-story former
courtroom is used as an experimental theater
and lecture hall by a community arts group.*

*Bulfinch Square has been home to the firm of Graham Gund Architects since 1985. Two former courtrooms are used as
large studios, while judges' chambers and jury rooms accommodate support and administrative functions.*

The courthouse buildings required extensive repairs and reconstruction to restore their dignity and create viable office space. Extensive research made it possible to re-create much of the ornamental plaster detailing that had been lost, as well as to reproduce accurate paint colors and finishes, including decorative stenciling.

This contemporary vacation residence abstracts and exaggerates the expansive roofs and shingle-style vernacular of Fisher's Island's large-scale summer homes. Its dramatic expression, in which roof and wall become one, grows up and out of the landscape, transcending issues of scale.

Dormers of various shapes and sizes punctuate the roofhouse and express a space within. The largest space is the living room: here an apselike dormer frames views up and down the coast. A two-story vertical dormer encloses the stair hall, while a freestanding face appears to have slid off the roof, defining the end of a ground-floor terrace. The portico gives way to a ship's ladder, which climbs the roof to a widow's walk.

The sloped site serves as an appropriate base for the curving house, which rises above the crest of the hill, sprouting white dormers like sails on a horizon in a playful celebration of summer and island living.

PATTERSON RESIDENCE

FISHER'S ISLAND, NEW YORK

A freestanding fireplace serves both the living and dining rooms, whose dormered windows shape and expand the house's simple volume.

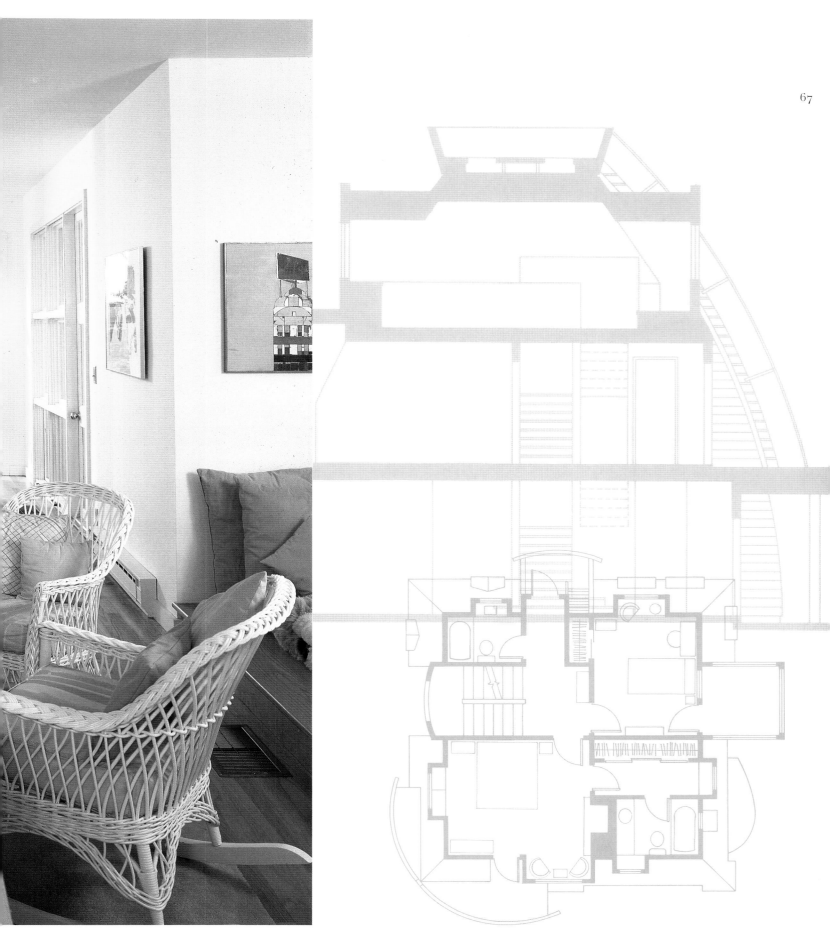

The regularly spaced, traditional windows in the living room of the Patterson residence open to views of Long Island Sound.

Gridded glazed walls frame the view from the dining room. The dining terrace is framed by a displaced dormer face, which seems to have fallen off the roof.

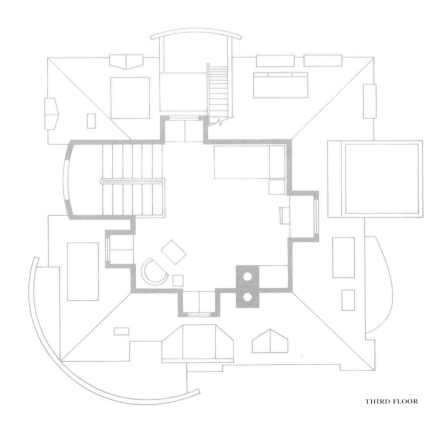

THIRD FLOOR

This country house for an equestrian family is sited against a backdrop of rolling fields and distant hills. The house is laid out around a central garden courtyard, expressing itself in the idiom of a stable with simple, traditional materials including cedar shingles and wood trim. Its cluster of shapes—gabled peaks and towers—encloses the courtyard, creating a protected space, in contrast to the openness of the untouched surrounding pastureland.

A gabled facade with oriel window marks the main entrance, where two garage bays, like sentinels, flank a narrow arched passageway leading to the courtyard beyond. At the far end of the courtyard is an octagonal tower whose base provides formal entrance to the house. The lantern of this tower provides a view from the tamed garden space to the natural landscape beyond.

The interior of the house is informal, spacious, and light filled. Most first floor rooms have double-height ceilings, which echo the shape of exterior gables, and expansive windows, which frame views of the landscape.

Rooms flow in linear fashion from one to the next, each having access to the courtyard core.

The master bedroom suite sits above the garage in a location that is both prominent (with its oriel window) and private. Stairs that bridge the main entrance passage lead past the suite and provide a circulation route that allows the family to circumnavigate the house without going outdoors.

NESBEDA RESIDENCE

HARVARD, MASSACHUSETTS

*The courtyard, entered through an arched passage-
way, provides both an outdoor living space and a
formal entrance to the Nesbeda house.*

*The library/study has the same octagonal form as
the tower that rises out of the courtyard.*

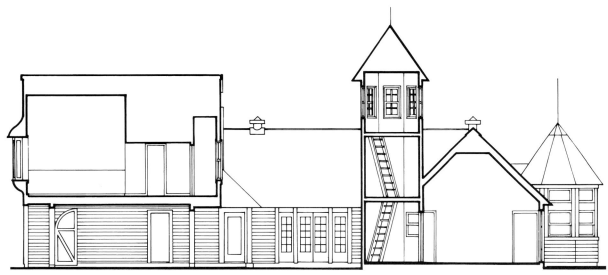

The kitchen work spaces float within the larger volume,
which includes a dining and family area.

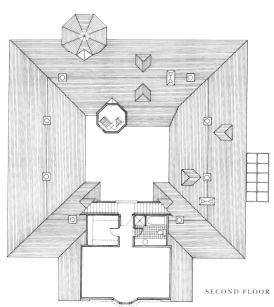

SECOND FLOOR

French doors lead to the living room, which flows into the entrance area at the base of the tower.

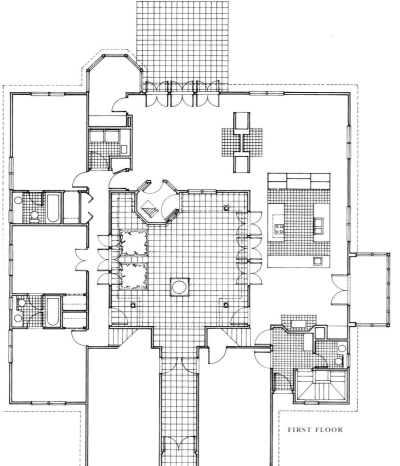

FIRST FLOOR

The circulation system around the house is completed by two staircases that meet at the master suite.

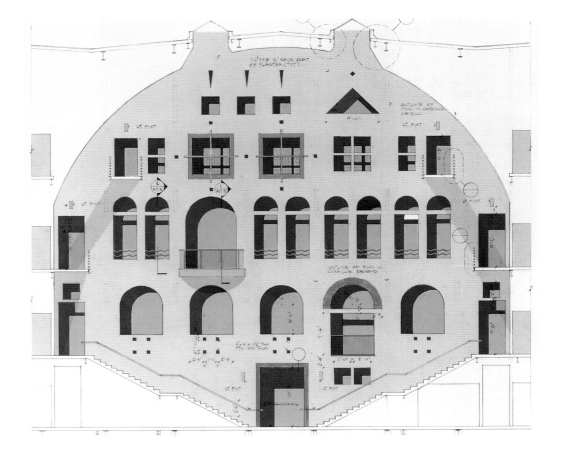

A dramatic four-story central atrium becomes a metaphorical theater, providing a stage set for the activity of The School-House residents.

The school's original two-story, central stair hall has been expanded to four stories and capped by skylights to animate the space with light and shadow. On one side of the space, a huge arched wall, alluding to a giant proscenium or theater house, is punctuated with rectangular, square, arched, and triangular windows to allow an exchange of light and a framing of views between the atrium and apartment galleries. On the other side of the atrium, open balconies provide direct access to apartment units and serve as a backdrop for Philip Grausman's "A Roost of Turkeys," which serves as actors or audience depending on the viewer's point of view. Such ambiguities between "stage" and "house," "actors" and "audience" add layers of interest and heighten the sense of drama within the space.

THE SCHOOL-HOUSE ON MONUMENT SQUARE

CHARLESTOWN, MASSACHUSETTS

All apartment entries face the courtyard. The open relationship between the light-filled circulation core and the apartment doors strengthens the sense of community.

The school's former triple vaulted auditorium is divided into six apartments, all of which incorporate architectural details from the ceiling.

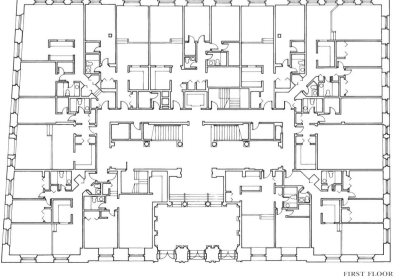

FIRST FLOOR

Art figured prominently in the conversion of this former Beacon Hill ballroom, whose owners wanted to create a home they could share with their extensive art collection. The dramatic two-story space, which explodes with light and air and art is situated behind a conservatively understated facade.

A central, double-height living space sits at the core, preserving the monumentality of the original room and, in essence, creating a house within a house. The living room (the little house within the bigger ballroom house) is enclosed by a second-story catwalk with a maple trellis railing and by two opposing, freestanding end walls, or toast walls, so-called for their shape and color.

The big house/little house juxtaposition is not the only reading intended for the space. The toast walls can either be seen as internal to the little house within the big house or as external walls fronting an outdoor space, as in a European courtyard. This playful reversal of scale and space creates tension and challenges the imagination.

One enters the space through a double-height, elliptical foyer, which is ringed above by an open second-story balcony. The entry floor, an elegant swirl of exotic wood inlay designed by Al Held, makes an exuberant greeting gesture, establishing that something unexpected is happening beyond and setting the stage for the celebration of art within.

COHEN RESIDENCE

BOSTON, MASSACHUSETTS

Visual and spatial connections to smaller living areas, such as the study, music alcove, and dining room are made through punched openings in the toast walls or through other gestures, such as transparent trellis railings and a grove of columns, which help establish the hierarchy of spaces in the Cohen residence.

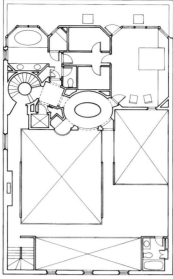

SECOND FLOOR

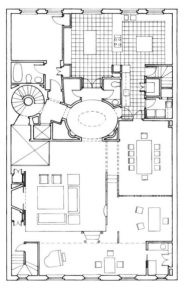

FIRST FLOOR

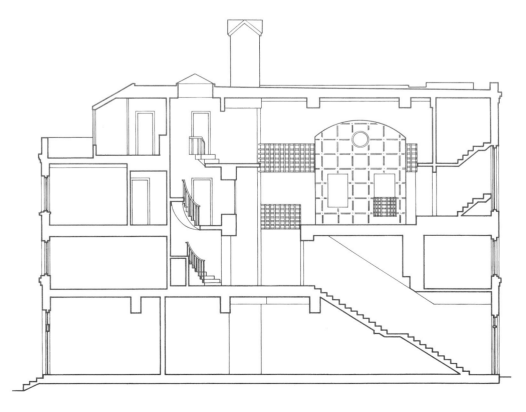

Large public and smaller private spaces are clearly delineated in the floor plans. The section illustrates the vertical circulation from the street.

The inlaid floor, designed by Al Held, provides a dramatic
introduction to the house. Its pattern is one of sinuous
curves overlaying grids like those found elsewhere in the house.

Plimoth Plantation is an outdoor living history museum, whose program of "first-person interpretation" transports visitors through time to the Plimoth Colony in the year 1627. The visitor center acts both as a gatehouse and as a place of temporal transition, in which visitors begin the figurative journey back in time to the seventeenth century Pilgrim village and Indian settlement beyond.

The building's simple, square, courtyard form recalls the imagery of the New England barn in deliberate contrast to the village grouping of the plantation's main exhibit. Massive barrel-shaped columns mark the entry, defining the interior courtyard and supporting the large, pitched roof. Dormers, cupolas, and an octagonal observation tower punctuate the roof.

The interior is organized to facilitate a three-part sequence of orientation, departure, and return. Upon arrival, visitors proceed to a theater to view an orientation film and to an exhibit space to view historic artifacts. They then ascend a tower stair to the lantern for a view of Plymouth harbor, with its symbolic connection to the Pilgrim's arrival, before departing on a tour of the plantation village. Returning through the building enables visitors to stop at the gift shop, dine, and re-view exhibits before leaving the museum.

PLIMOTH PLANTATION VISITOR CENTER

PLYMOUTH, MASSACHUSETTS

The protected courtyard provides a comfortable gathering place in nearly all seasons as well as necessary overflow space during peak visitor seasons. Visitors see an orientation movie, view artifacts in the exhibition hall, and then proceed to the tower, which overlooks Plymouth harbor.

FIRST FLOOR

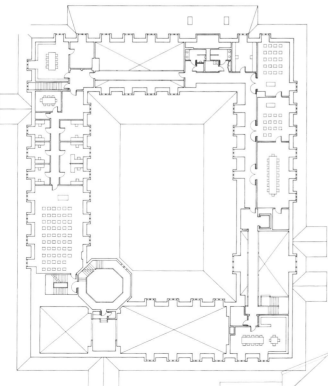

SECOND FLOOR

A porch off the dining room affords a view of Plymouth Bay through the massive columns that support the large roof.

The entry connects the visitor areas with the library, workshops, and administrative spaces above.

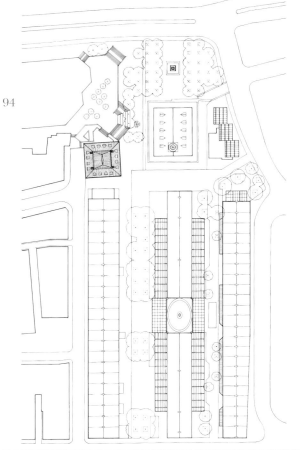

Set at the crossroads of historic Faneuil Hall, Quincy Market, and State Street, One Faneuil Hall Square occupies one of the most contextually complex sites in downtown Boston. The site demands a well-composed object building that allows Faneuil Hall to retain its place at center stage in the marketplace composition. The play between vernacular and contemporary architectural language is the defining concept for this project.

Seven stories tall, the new building acts as a transition element in location, scale, and detailing, mediating between the high-rise towers of glass and stone veneer and the smaller historic structures of brick and gray granite. Its simple massing and contemporary expression relate equally to old and new, high and low, large and small, vehicular and pedestrian—abstracting and inverting ideas that are central to the downtown towers and the traditional buildings surrounding the marketplace. As a piece of marketplace architecture itself, the building becomes a highly animated object, like an overscaled kiosk that transforms itself from day to night.

The primary surface material is a warm New England granite. Bold surface patterning in accents of granite, travertine, and marble and a varied fenestration recall the architecture of adjacent historic buildings and visually lighten the massing by breaking up the facade into a loosely defined, almost ambiguous cornice, middle, and base. Windows of varied shapes and sizes (square, round, and arched) are arranged in vertical stacks and horizontal bands, like the belt courses on neighboring buildings. The fenestration provides a sense of scale and allows multiple readings, which heighten the visual cadence of the building's four facades, treating them like treasure within a jewel box created by the anonymous enclosure of skyscrapers.

ONE FANEUIL HALL SQUARE

BOSTON, MASSACHUSETTS

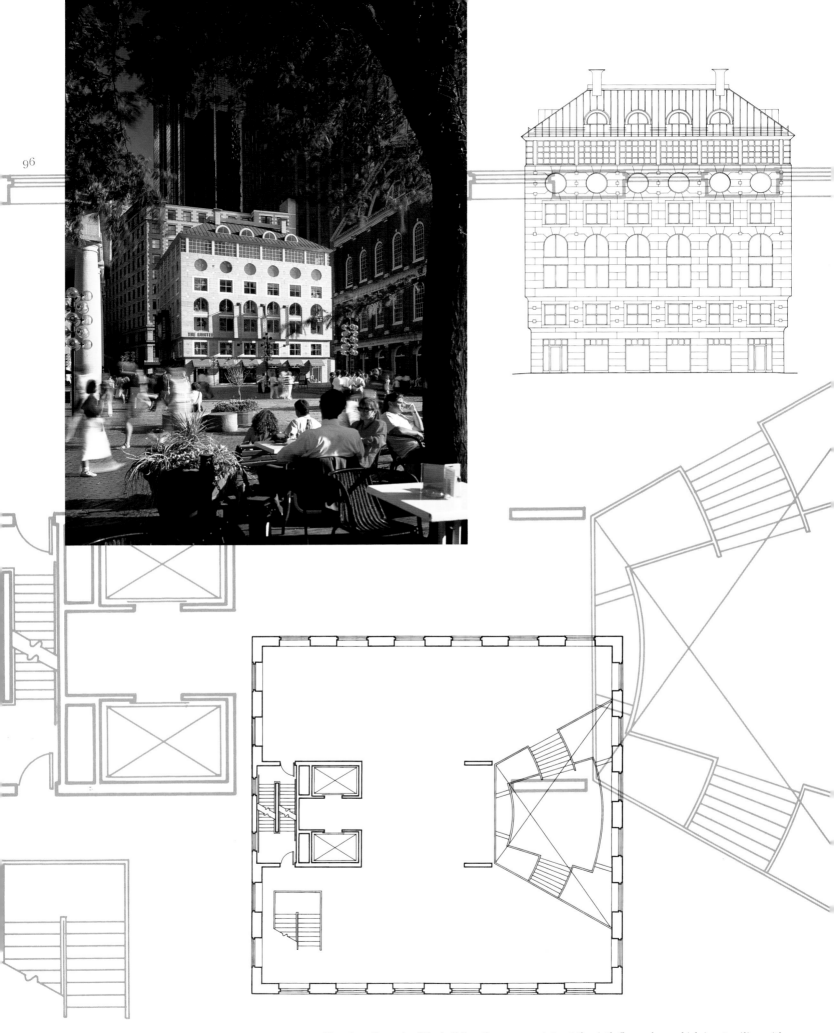

To reduce the scale of the building the masonry stops at the sixth floor, above which is a pavilion with glass sides. Patterns in the stone continue the verticality of the columns down the facade. The joints in the exterior stonework are detailed to resemble those found in other buildings in the marketplace.

CONNECTICUT COLLEGE

NEW LONDON, CONNECTICUT

Recognizing the powerful role of first impressions in shaping a prospective student's enthusiasm for an institution and that the decision about whether to attend a school is made within moments after arriving on campus, Connecticut College's new admissions building carefully choreographs the experience of arrival and introduction to reveal much about the spirit of the college. The building reflects the intimacy and stature of the school, with an architectural expression that is at once dignified and welcoming.

Its form, evocative of a turn-of-the-century country house, speaks to the building's role as a special place on campus that literally and figuratively mediates between the large academic buildings and the smaller-scaled residential neighborhood off campus.

The building, with its four corner towers, is a symbolic gateway through which visitors pass to gain a formal introduction to the campus. The main entry is located behind the building on the south facade where visitor parking has been hidden out of sight of the entry drive. A simple plan organizes the interior, highlighting a gracious arrival sequence and procession through the building to the grand campus view beyond. An entry porch flows into a reception hall with grand stairway and then into a two-story cathedral-ceilinged great room. An outdoor terrace on the north side of the building serves as spill-over space during busy interviewing periods.

The great room, a waiting room for prospective students and their families, is the symbolic and functional heart of the new building. The room is flanked by twin fireplaces, positioned to create two distinct seating groups in an atmosphere of homelike warmth and comfort. Large windows frame expansive views of the campus, while an oversized, arched dormer in the two-story space brings light into a second-story walkway that connects the corner tower interview rooms.

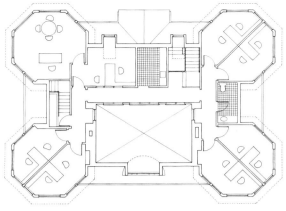

SECOND FLOOR

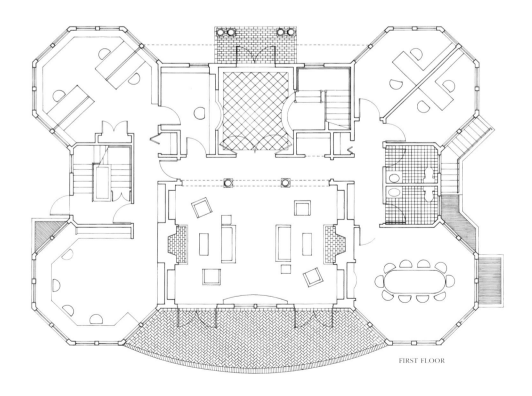

FIRST FLOOR

Twin fireplaces define two smaller seating areas within the large room that serves as a central welcoming space.
The use of large rounded windows adds a dynamic quality to the interior of the admissions building.

LINCOLN LIBRARY

LINCOLN, MASSACHUSETTS

The residential scale and character of the town and existing library are key to the design of a substantial new addition to an 1883 Queen Anne–style building. The new addition recognizes the building's role as a community library and important place of discovery for children, expressing in its free interpretation of the playful Queen Anne style the adventure, excitement, and mystery found in books.

Taking cues from the asymmetry of the original building, with its eccentric roof peaks, tower, turrets, and gabled ends, the new addition is conceived as a pair of pavilions. The two, which in massing and form are similar to the 1883 structure, are linked together and to the original library by a semitransparent bridge element constructed of metal and glass. The square pavilion wings are topped with hipped roofs and are framed by a pair of tall end walls with stepped gables.

The two new wings are further related to the original building through an exuberant use of decorative masonry, which recalls but does not replicate the existing patterning.

Inside, the expanded building is organized around a new circulation spine, which, on the entry level, relocates circulation and reference functions off the new entry foyer. The spine provides access to the "link" connector and other library spaces, including the stacks, and serves as an organizer of an otherwise asymmetrical plan. The second level of the new wings (the main level of the existing library) houses an expanded children's collection whose two reading rooms have been conceived as highly animated spaces, with vaulted ceilings, decorative trusswork, and playful window shapes. An octagonal room tucked into one of the building's new turrets serves as a storytelling room for small children.

The playful details of the exterior and interior treatment of the addition to Lincoln Library reinterpret the exuberance of the original 1883 decoration.

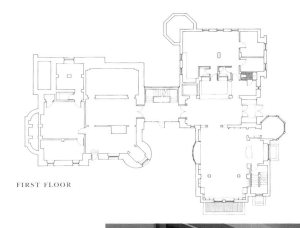

FIRST FLOOR

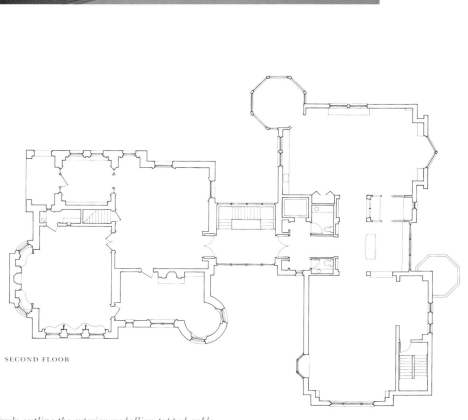

SECOND FLOOR

The trusses freely outline the exterior medallion-topped gable,
which forms the end of the children's reading room.

Known in an earlier life as 15 New Chardon Street, One Bowdoin Square is neither a new structure nor a rehabilitation. Rather, it is a building re-made. The foundation and frame of a yellow-brick 1972 seven-story structure has been given new life by means of a four-story addition and dramatic new skin.

At the base of the building is Cardinal Cushing Park, a contemporaneous urban pocket park, which, like the original building, appeared stark and worn. The park, too, is transformed, replacing cold concrete walls and seating with new landscaping, brick paving, and cast iron benches.

A dramatic new entryway, cut in the shape of a drawn curtain, exploits the intimate connection between the park and the building. Outlined in alternating ribbons of polished and rough granite, the entrance embraces the park, drawing it in to a large two-story lobby. A sense of grandness in the lobby is heightened by a vaulted ceiling, which is painted a celestial azure blue and studded with bronze spheres.

Organized with a base, shaft, and crown, the facades of One Bowdoin Square are charged with an energy that sets them apart from the surrounding gray brick and concrete government structures. Though the building is clad in traditional brick and granite, the bold patterning of masonry and fenestration make it highly animated. Oversized windows provide views and abundant natural light, and add variety to the building surface. Round windows separate the base of the building from the middle, while square windows mark the middle and allow the dramatic cornice to float.

At the building's crown is a fiberglass reinforced concrete cornice, which flares out eight feet from the building's edge, supporting a pyramidal copper roof. The cornice gives the top of the building a sense of importance (which could not be achieved by tapering or shaping in other ways because of height restrictions), and provides a ceiling for the outdoor space below.

ONE BOWDOIN SQUARE

BOSTON, MASSACHUSETTS

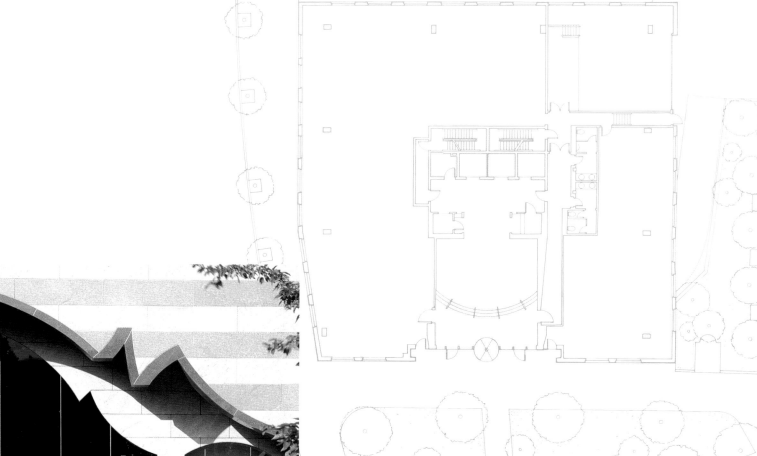

The layered edges of the entry to One Bowdoin Square resemble a pulled back stage curtain, revealing the vaulted forms of the lobby with its star-studded blue ceiling.

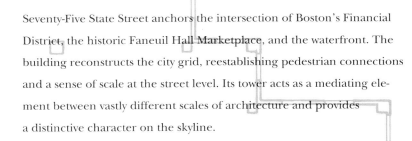

Seventy-Five State Street anchors the intersection of Boston's Financial District, the historic Faneuil Hall Marketplace, and the waterfront. The building reconstructs the city grid, reestablishing pedestrian connections and a sense of scale at the street level. Its tower acts as a mediating element between vastly different scales of architecture and provides a distinctive character on the skyline.

At street level, the building's scale, texture, and color reflect that of neighboring historic buildings and create variety and richness. Where the building meets the street, a six-story cap is maintained, extending a low building height along State Street from the Old State House to its termination at the edge of the waterfront. The building's facade is articulated with a one-story stone base, punched masonry openings, and cornices reintroduced in a contemporary manner.

Though the building fills the 60,000-square-foot site, the tower is set back from the street to disconnect the mass from the pedestrian environment and to restore the sense of scale. A large-scale layering of patterns, colors, and textures demands participation and attention and creates a three-dimensional quality with apparent depth of field, while allowing for the use of a curtain wall construction system. Bay windows create a vertical emphasis and allow for the creation of a dozen corner offices on each floor. To maintain a sense of scale in the tower, it is stepped at 125 feet and at 260 feet.

The building's six-story, skylighted interior great hall is a transition space between the street and the office tower and is important to the building's role as a provider of pedestrian connections. Lined with retail shops, this animated arcade provides passage from Faneuil Hall and Merchants Row to Liberty Square, in the tradition of great European galleries. A cross axis also permits and encourages pedestrian use from the low-scale historic area near the harbor to the high-rise area immediately to the west, literally bringing the street grid and city fabric through the building.

The main entry is flanked by two towers indicating the entry to the building beyond. The materials, palette, and small-scale patterning on the six story building containing the main entrance to 75 State Street relate to the pedestrian experience. The 31-story office tower, set back from the street, has enlarged patterning meant to be seen from a distance.

The processional entrance from State Street passes through the skylighted great hall and culminates in an arch-shaped lobby at the base of the taller building.

Built in the tradition of the grand resort hotel, the Golden Eagle Lodge stands before its White Mountains backdrop, at once enhancing and being enhanced by the dramatic silhouette. The hotel's expressive building form, with its broad sloping roof, tower peaks, roof valleys, and crescent footprint echoes the organic shapes of the mountains.

Constructed of wood and fieldstone and clad in shingles, the lodge bends gently to enclose a front lawn and entry courtyard. An archway, which penetrates the hotel's main facade, leads pedestrians by footpath to the outside of the crescent and to the new Waterville Valley Town Square beyond. This outer facade follows the crest of the hill. It is punctuated by a series of towers, which define the large scale of the exterior viewed from across the lake and from the town square.

An overall sense of informality is heightened through elements of varied scale, such as the dormers that dot the roofline like houses on a hillside, and a broad, front rocking porch reminiscent of those on country inns.

Inside, a spacious two-story lobby has two large fireplaces and a view to the lake. Guest units are arranged as apartments with kitchens and living areas.

GOLDEN EAGLE LODGE

WATERVILLE VALLEY, NEW HAMPSHIRE

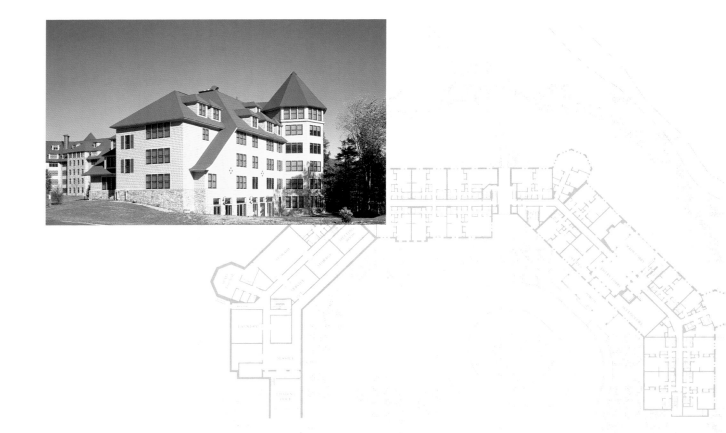

120

The plan of the Golden Eagle Lodge follows the line of the ridge above the pond.
Towers punctuate the segmented facade like knuckles on a fist.

122

WATERVILLE VALLEY TOWN SQUARE

WATERVILLE VALLEY, NEW HAMPSHIRE

Waterville Valley's Town Square provides a physical and emotional focus for this sprawling year-round ski and recreational resort in the White Mountains of New Hampshire. Working with the spectacular mountain scenery as a backdrop, the design of the new center speaks to the history, spirit, and simple beauty of the natural environment in this rural New England setting.

The town square adopts the traditional New England village as its model. The village consists of a cluster of five freestanding, white clapboard buildings, which draw upon the simple design elements of New England mill towns, Puritan settlements, and Shaker villages. The building forms are assertions of human order in the landscape, finding beauty through proportion and scale, and strength through repetition and simplicity.

The individual buildings form two large courtyards, one which opens onto Corcoran's Pond, the other onto a rambling brook. In the manner of European resort towns, the courtyards are the core of the new town square. These community spaces accommodate vendors and performers in warmer weather and sleigh rides in winter.

All buildings are connected by a ground floor arcade and a second level open walkway. The lower two levels (one of which steps down the hill) house retail shops, a restaurant, post office, and nightclubs. Above a layer of office space, the square's upper three levels contain staff housing arranged in duplexes and triplexes.

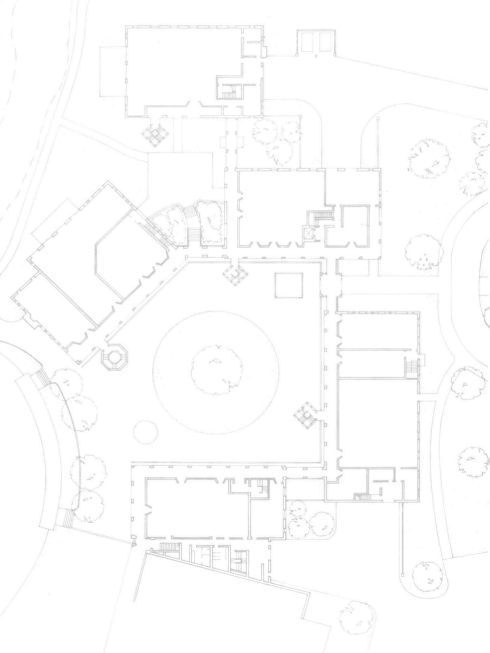

The mixed use aspect of Waterville Valley Town Square is masked by its differing window forms.

In contrast to the informality of nearby Golden Eagle Lodge, the design of the Town Square is formal, with more regularity in its plan, fenestration, and facade materials.

WESTMINSTER SCHOOL

SIMSBURY, CONNECTICUT

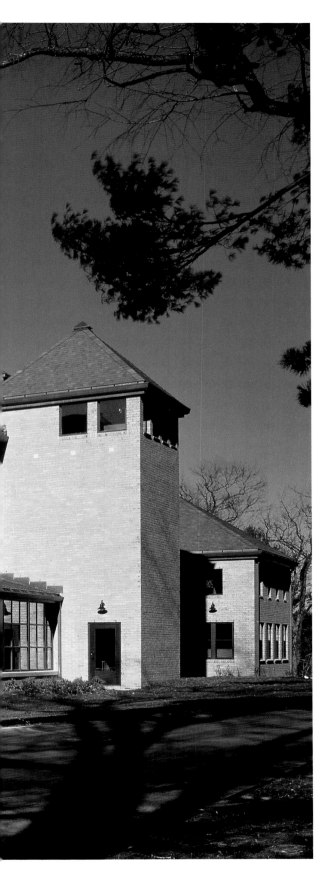

Drama, festivity, and excitement have moved to the center of the Westminster School campus in the new Centennial Center. A twin-towered entry facade speaks to the building's theatrical nature, with its animated expression, Shakespearean balconies, and overscaled two-story arched entry. The facade creates a backdrop for a prominent new campus green placed in an area once blighted by parking, and frames views on three levels of the central campus quadrangle. Sloping roof forms with dormer skylights and brick walls in buff and terra-cotta tones reflect the school's Tudor vernacular and integrate the building into the campus.

An understanding of actor/audience dynamics informs the design of the theater space. With a tier-to-tier width of 32 feet, and with the farthest seat only 40 feet from the apron of the stage, the scale is intimate—not intimidating—and the spirit communal, allowing actors and audience to share in and reinforce each others' excitement. The courtyard form allows for an animated interior expression, since people, not blank walls, enclose the space. The theater meets a range of audience requirements, from seating an intimate lecture group of 100 to accommodating up to 400 people for special all-school events. Its horseshoe shape and tiered balconies allows the size of the audience and the perceived scale of the space to be adjusted upward or downward by simply opening or closing the balcony spaces and by turning the lights on or off.

The theater's detailing speaks to the school's heritage and pride. Rich woodwork, recessed paneling, round columns, and coffered ceilings evoke a deep sense of tradition and contribute to the acoustical richness of the space.

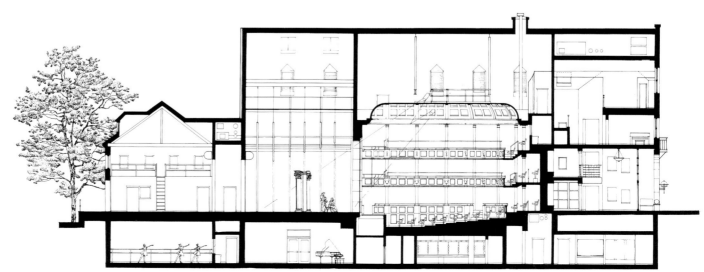

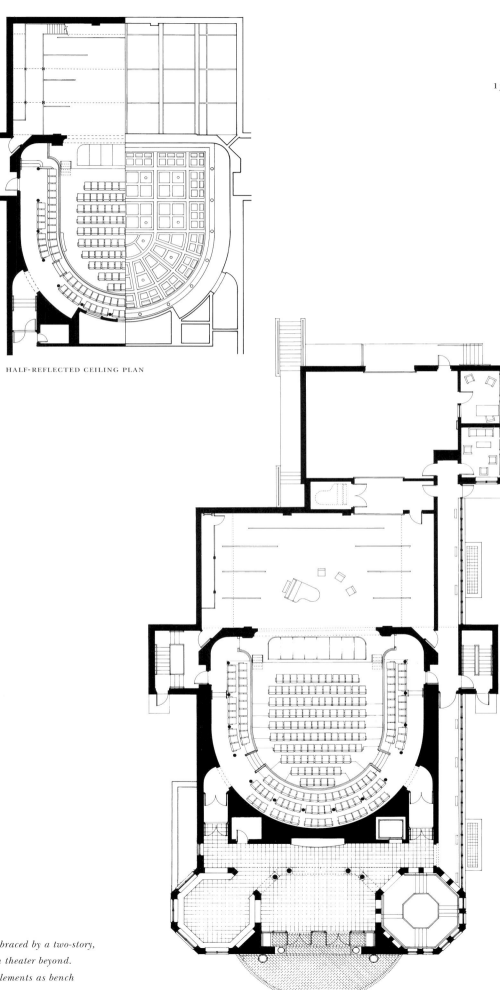

131

HALF-REFLECTED CEILING PLAN

Upon entry, a visitor to this performing arts center is embraced by a two-story, balconied lobby, which hints at the grandeur of the main theater beyond. The building addresses the needs of students with such elements as bench alcoves, which provide a place for private conversation.

FIRST FLOOR

The theater experience at Westminster School is enlivened for actors and audience alike by the intimacy created by their close physical relationship.

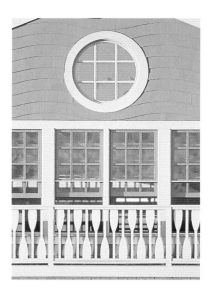

Located on the banks of the Charles River, this new boat-house captures the spirit of a century-old architectural tradition by making connections to the boathouses of Harvard, Boston University, and neighboring rowing clubs.

Architectural connections to the nearby boat-houses are explicitly made through the use of familiar forms from the past, such as towers at each of the building's four corners, a broad roof (which slopes down to one story on all four facades), dormers, shingle siding, and porches.

Playfully animated details echo a nautical theme. The wave shingle patterning on the dormers, and oar-shaped balusters along the balconies are innovations used to distinguish the new boathouse from its older neighbors.

Inside, the building contains six boat bays on the first level and weight and exercise rooms, locker rooms, coaches' offices, and a balcony for spectators on the second.

The simplicity of form and the necessary dependence on the quality of craftsmanship treats the construction of the building like the crafting of a boat and the architecture like a timeless and utilitarian reflection of the sport.

NORTHEASTERN UNIVERSITY

BOSTON, MASSACHUSETTS

HENDERSON BOATHOUSE

The sense of arrival at both the land and water facades is heightened by the symmetrical arrangement of portal elements.

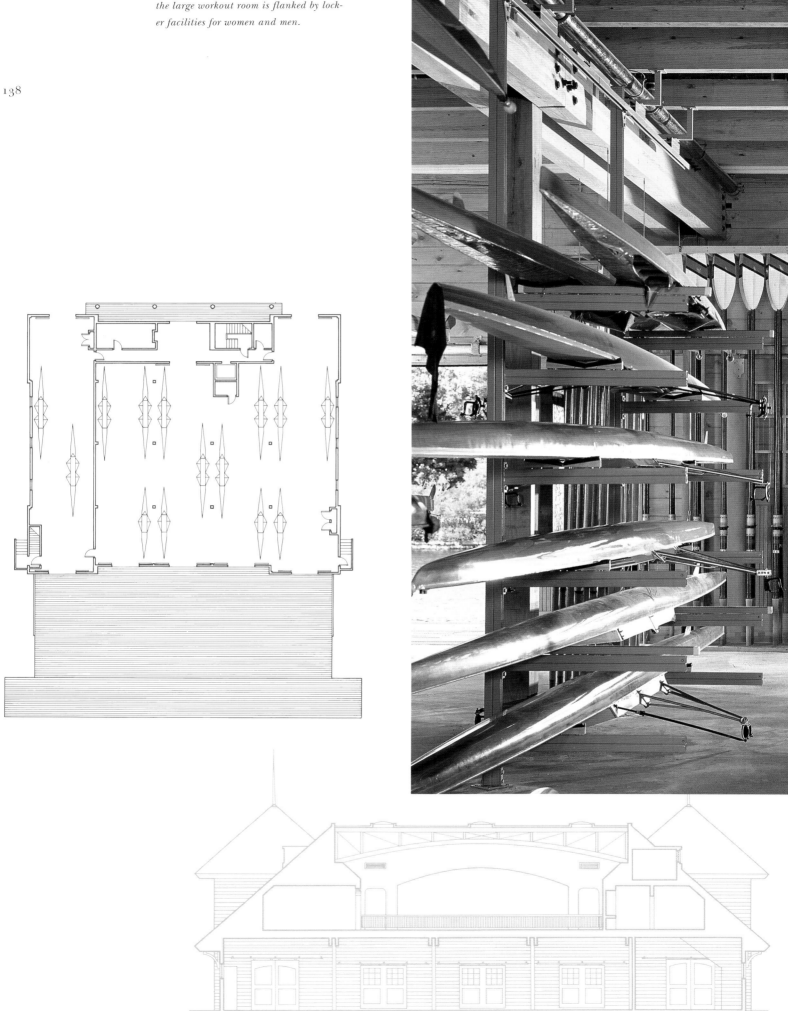

The taut and precise wood framing of the boat bays complements minimalist beauty of the rowing shells. On the second floor, the large workout room is flanked by locker facilities for women and men.

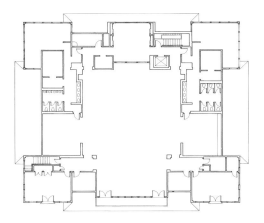

Set back from a secluded country lane, this residence was conceived of as a cluster of pavilions integrated within a very private, gardenlike landscape. The pavilions—house, garage, and toolshed—serve as sculptural elements in the larger framework of the landscape, at the same time creating between them a more internalized landscape in the form of an entry court.

The intimate yet grand feeling of this moderately sized house of 3,750 square feet is perhaps its most charming as well as intriguing feature. The massing and scale give it the feeling of being larger than it is, as does the unique floor plan. The various rooms are organized as distinct spaces clustered around a central two–story hall, each room having a different relationship with the hall and with each other. The positioning of rooms on the diagonal and the use of special figural shapes, e.g. the square and the octagon, also contribute to the feeling of spaciousness, and allow each room a unique orientation and view into the landscape.

SHAPLEIGH RESIDENCE

LADUE, MISSOURI

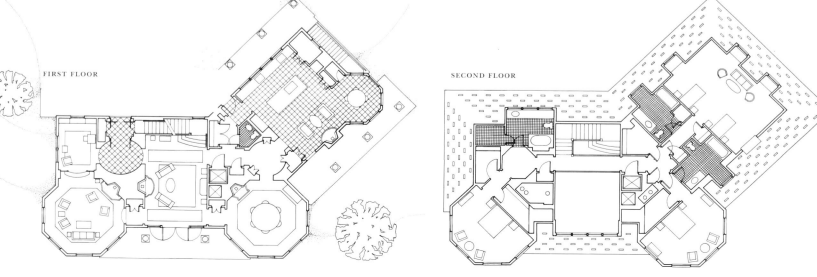

FIRST FLOOR

SECOND FLOOR

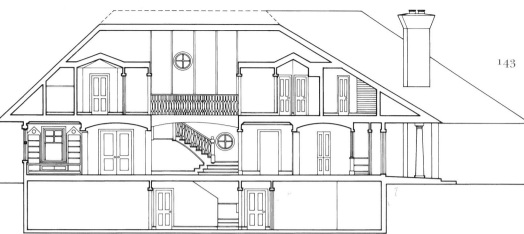

The welcoming shape of the entry facade is articulated with small-scale elements. On the opposite side of the house, large turrets and porches burst forth into the landscape.

The living room incorporates one of four specially designed fireplace mantels; it is patterned after a sombrero. The dining room mantel features an urn, the kitchen a teapot, and the hall the Eye of Knowledge.

The hall extends all the way through the house from floor to roof.

The principal facade of the Inn at Harvard fills a former void and creates a needed ceremonial end for Harvard Square. The placement of this facade at the narrow end of the site led to the courtyard plan and allows the reinterpretation of the Harvard House as an inn.

The inn's main facade at Quincy Street is strong and formal and provides a focal point for the Square in the manner of other important Harvard buildings through the superimposition of large-scale ordering elements. It borrows and abstracts architectural elements, including pilasters, capitals, bases, and an entablature from the public faces of Lehman Hall, Eliot House, and other Harvard landmarks. The implied large-scale reading of the Quincy Street facade responds to the urban scale of the Square.

Inside, the focal point of the inn is the four-story grand courtyard space, which serves as lobby and living room. The fully skylighted courtyard uses fragile interior materials with an exterior vocabulary. The dynamic daylight and this unexpected juxtaposition create a lively animation in this gathering space. The living room functions as a multiple-use space, symbolically reinforcing its connection to the common rooms of the Harvard Houses.

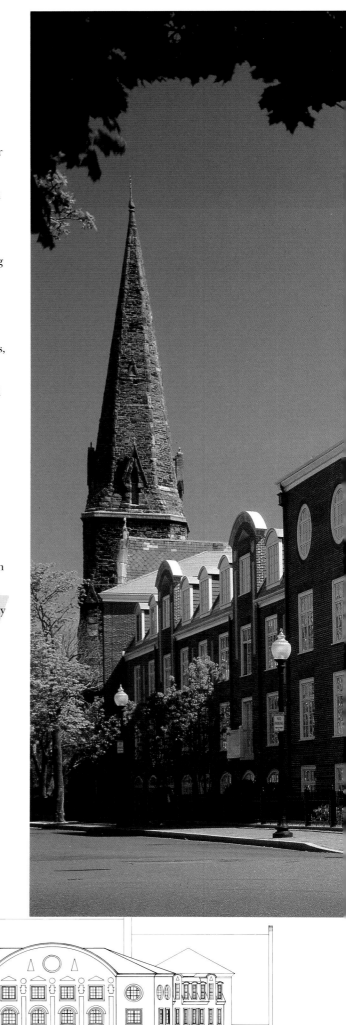

THE INN AT HARVARD

CAMBRIDGE, MASSACHUSETTS

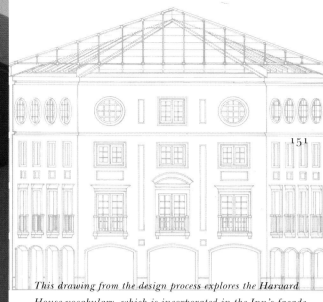

This drawing from the design process explores the Harvard House vocabulary, which is incorporated in the Inn's facade.

A skylight covers the central courtyard at The Inn at Harvard, which functions as living room, library, and dining space. The filtered light reinforces the impression of the space as a frescoed Italian courtyard.

The large doors of some guest rooms face the courtyard,
heightening the sense of the space as an outdoor room.

A lyrical flow of elements gives spirited definition to the facades of the new Boston Ballet. The building's lively patterning of windows in different sizes and shapes expresses the movement and grace of ballet dance and allows the activity inside to be brought out to the street, where music and motion engage and delight passersby.

The overscaled windows stack up in ways that, like dancers, seem to defy gravity and weight and create a childlike feeling, which helps reduce the scale of the building. The building's prominent cornice is cut away at the front corners to create a for-

mal entrance facade whose scale and character are sympathetic to the surrounding historic residential neighborhood and whose sense of ceremony helps establish a physical identity for the ballet company within the city fabric.

Inside, the building is organized around a central open stair hall, which ascends in a fluid spiral motion through the four-story volume. The stair links a large stagelike landing in the double-height entry lobby with rehearsal studios and administrative offices on the upper levels, encouraging the mingling of staff, dancers, students, and their families. Diffused glass windows behind the stair allow shadows of dancers and indirect natural light to penetrate through to the building's core and animate the lobby theater.

At the rear of the building, dance studios stack up side by side behind the stair hall. The uppermost levels house a two-story Grand Studio, which at 50 x 100 feet is the size of the ballet's performance stage at Boston's Wang Center for the Performing Arts. In this studio, choreographers and dancers are able to rehearse full productions in the accurate scale of an actual production stage.

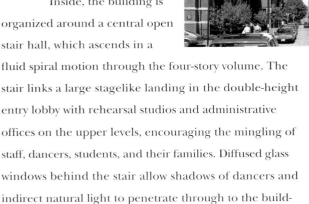

BOSTON BALLET

BOSTON, MASSACHUSETTS

The fenestration of the Boston Ballet building is designed to reveal the activity within and, through its composition, to create a feeling of the lightness and spirit of dance movement.

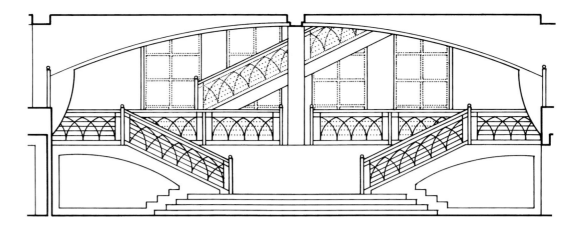

Sweeping overhead arches enclose the lobby space, giving the sense of a proscenium. Two small "Juliet" balconies hang from an open mezzanine that surrounds the lobby. The stair and lobby balconies are trimmed with a painted metal railing, which evokes the movement of dance. The railing's graceful overlapping arcs are set against horizontal bands that provide a referenced plane, just as the bars of sheet music do.

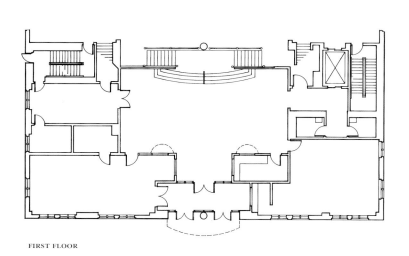

FIRST FLOOR

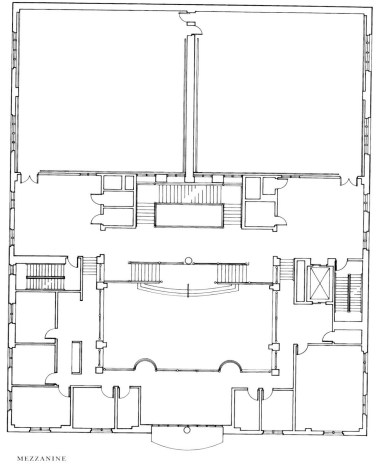

MEZZANINE

FIFTH FLOOR

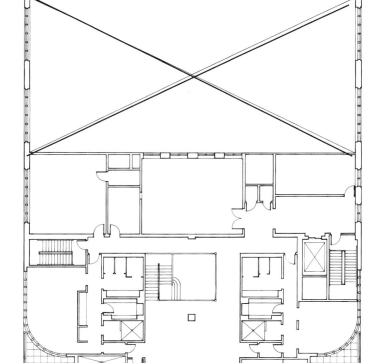

The Grand Studio, which occupies the top floor along with private dressing, exercise, and training rooms, is the signature space of the building.

The Village Commons at South Hadley provides a
new town center for this small college town in western
Massachusetts, whose original village retail strip was
devastated by competition from regional shopping malls.
The development revives the heart of the community
by creating an interdependent retail, commercial, and
residential core that reestablishes the importance of
the town center and draws people back to a forgotten
way of life.

The Village Commons creates the illusion of
a community that has evolved naturally over time.
Employing the characteristic New England notion of
simple block buildings fronting village streets and
yards, eleven three-story buildings line the town's main
street. Together, this street and a new street enclose
the village. Each building has a distinct character which
orients users and rein-
forces the sense that the
community has taken
shape over time. Entrances
on all sides of the village
encourage exploration and
discovery.

Architecturally,
the Village Commons mar-
ries the traditional and
the eccentric as an inven-
tion of style. Wood clap-
boards, pitched roofs, and modestly scaled windows and
doors recall the traditional townscape in a contemporary way. Each facade has a simple order, with added
elements such as bay windows, balconies, or arcades,
and playful wood details that allow the possibility of
multiple readings and add layers of visual interest.
These elements serve as focal points and provide visual
movement and a spirit of delight.

THE VILLAGE COMMONS

SOUTH HADLEY, MASSACHUSETTS

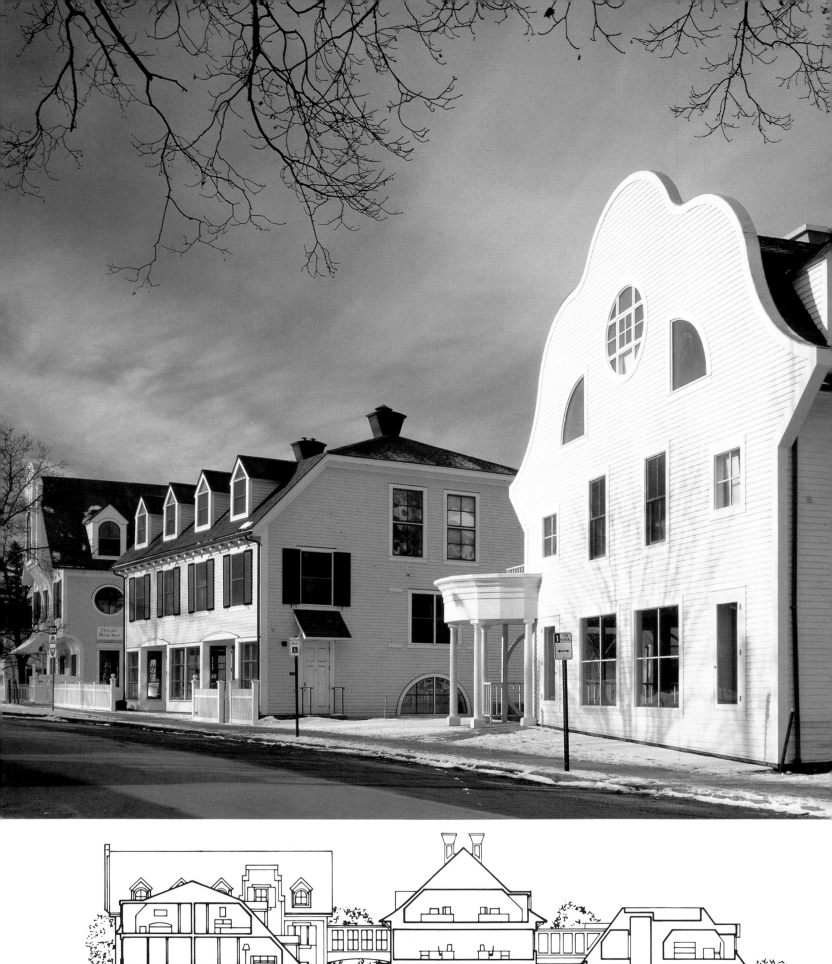
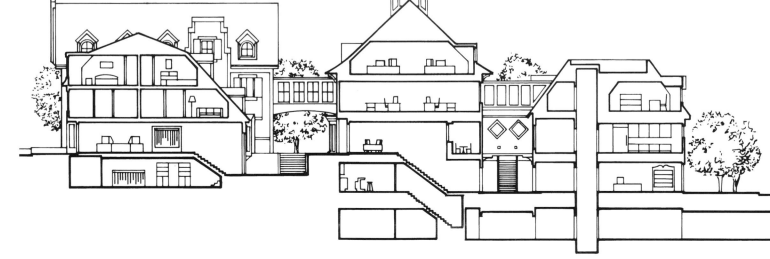

The buildings front on both the town common and a new street. They adapt to the steep slope of the site, providing a direct connection to grade from several levels. Parking is staggered on landscaped tiers. Service to the buildings is concealed and occurs at the lowest parking level where loading docks connect to a network of underground tunnels. Screening and isolating the service function allows the buildings to have public faces on all four facades.

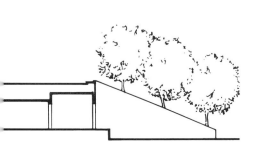

The spatial organization of the village assigns equal importance to buildings, courtyards, and pedestrian circulation. Pedestrians traverse the site through interconnected courtyards, each with a distinctive character and landscape. Second-floor bridge connections provide an additional means of circulation.

The facades of the buildings in the Village Commons incorporate a playful abstraction of elements found in New England towns.

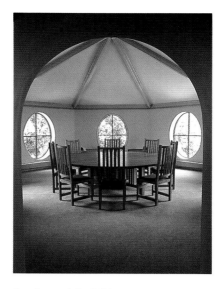

A substantial addition to two existing buildings (one the original library, the other an adjacent classroom building) creates a major new library and computer sciences center for Mount Holyoke College. The complex tells the story of the historical evolution of the library as a building genre and chronicles the century-long evolution of a campus landmark, whose history bears the mark of numerous periods of architecture.

The existing library tower, a strong symbol for the college community, marks the main entry to the building and houses a stair hall and lobby. Beyond it, the floors of a dark 1905 stack wing addition have been carved out to create a new light-filled courtyard center that organizes the functions and epochs of architecture that surround it. Its classical design makes reference to the pivotal role of the Renaissance in the evolution of the library and education and celebrates the diverse stylistic layers represented within Mount Holyoke's facility. Just as the tower is the symbolic marker of the library on campus, the courtyard is the symbolic center of the academic community, both spatially and historically. Appropriately, the courtyard sits at the crossroads between the route to the library's original 1870 cathedral-like reading room, whose great trussed space alludes to the ecclesiastical roots of library and education, and the new science and technology addition.

The new addition loosely interprets the collegiate Gothic style, using brick instead of stone to relate to the color and texture of the existing campus vernacular. Buttresses modulate the facade, but without the rigor and discipline of structural elements. Bays, which serve as interior reading spaces, give the otherwise anonymous box of books a distinctive library face.

MT. HOLYOKE COLLEGE WILLISTON LIBRARY

SOUTH HADLEY, MASSACHUSETTS

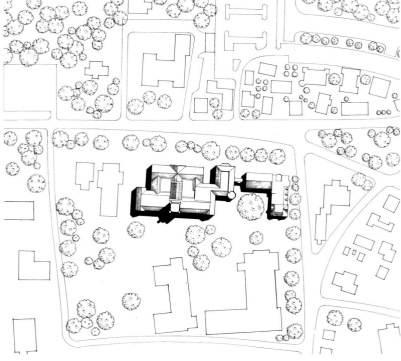

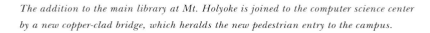

The addition to the main library at Mt. Holyoke is joined to the computer science center by a new copper-clad bridge, which heralds the new pedestrian entry to the campus.

The new courtyard transforms the original 1905 stack wing into the focal point of the renovated library. As originally constructed, the stack wing was a book-filled space surrounded by light; now it is a light-filled space surrounded by books. The two existing campus buildings—the original library and Dwight Hall—are joined by a new science library addition, indicated in yellow on the plan.

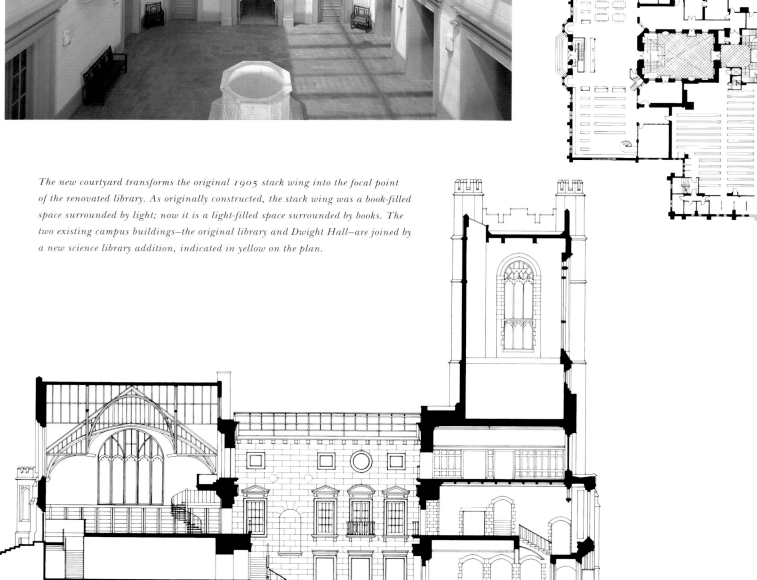

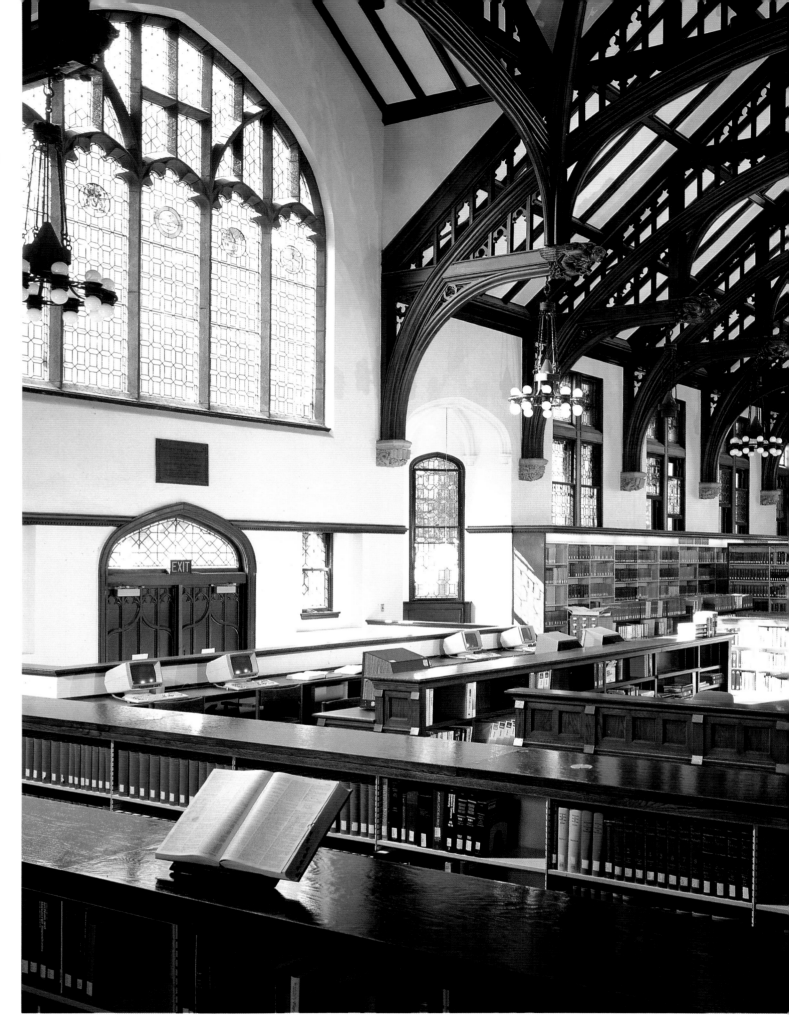

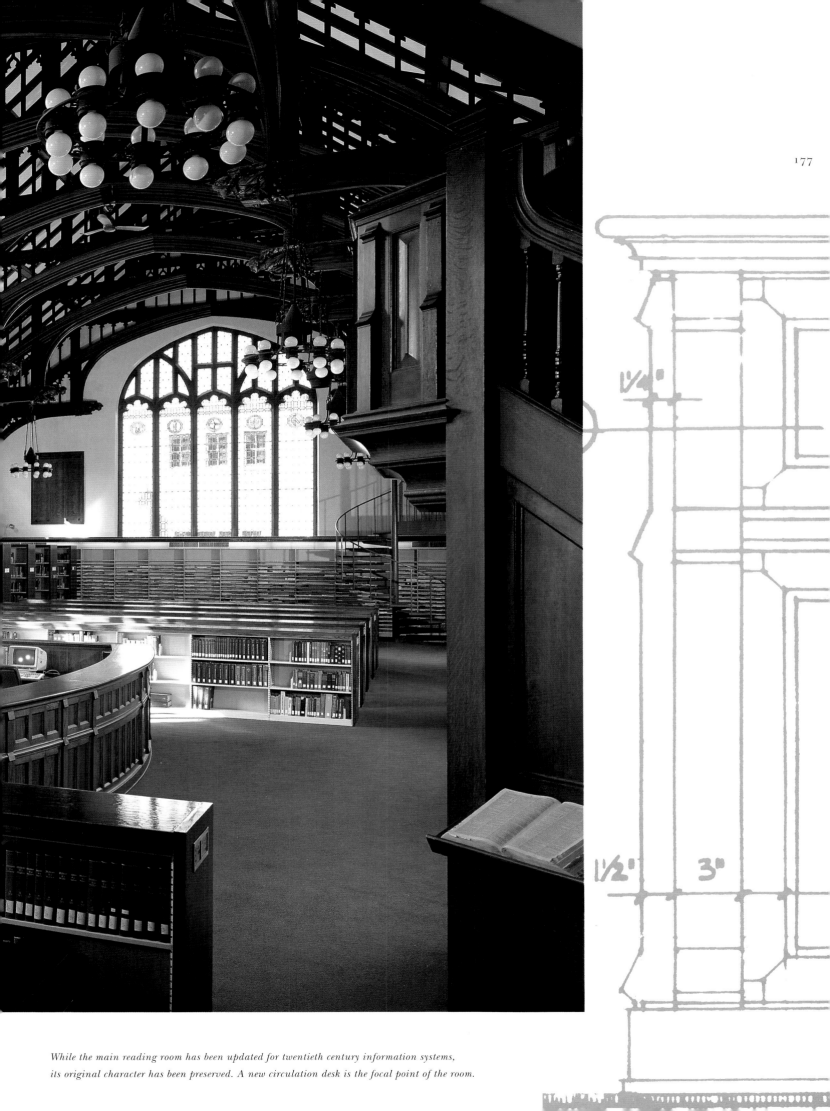

While the main reading room has been updated for twentieth century information systems,
its original character has been preserved. A new circulation desk is the focal point of the room.

THE LANSBURGH

WASHINGTON, D.C.

181

This large, mixed-use development anchors Washington's Pennsylvania Quarter, a new residential neighborhood and cultural district located downtown in the center of the capital's once-thriving retail core. The winning entry in a federally sponsored development competition, the project transformed a blighted monolithic commercial block into a cluster of more humanly scaled neighborhood pieces, representing a mix of residential, retail, and cultural arts space.

As required by the Pennsylvania Avenue Development Corporation, the design substantially reuses three existing buildings on site: the Lansburgh department store, the Anheuser Busch warehouse, and the S. S. Kresge store. The stylistic and functional diversity of these buildings provides an exciting melange of materials and textures.

Along 7th Street, an entirely new facade has a rhythmic series of brick bays, which expresses the building's residential function. The facade is broken into five vertical forms, each with a separate street expression, that allude to individual town houses and reflect the residential architecture of nearby Logan Circle with bowed fronts, angled bay windows, setbacks, belt courses, cornices, and a colorful variety of masonry patterns.

In addition to its other attractions, the Lansburgh incorporates a 450-seat live theater, which is the new home of the Shakespeare Company, formerly at the Folger Library on Capitol Hill. The entrance to the theater is located in one of the five subdivisions of the 7th Street facade. This section is distinguished from the others in its material and form, an octagonal column that extends the full height of the building.

The courtyard within the larger U-Shaped plan is terraced over the various theater and health club volumes located below. The facades overlooking the courtyard refer to each other with a series of balconies and bays, rather than to the street-side facades. This inner garden space ties the project together and provides a quiet retreat and sanctuary in the heart of the city.

The north and west elevations of the Lansburgh complex include three historic facades. Retail establishments along the ground level of the redeveloped site contribute to the newly created neighborhood.

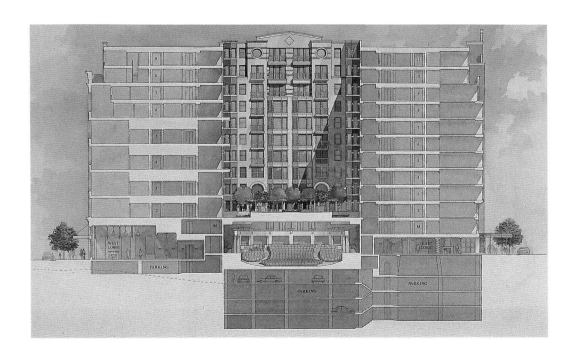

A terraced garden courtyard provides a lush, peaceful setting for the inward-facing units.
Its form flows in part from the volumes of the theater and health club below.

Boxes surround the seating of the Lansburgh Theater,
which is also ringed by a freestanding arcade. The theater
incorporates a substantial fly loft and orchestra pit and
can accommodate programs of drama, music, and dance.

*The residential lobby on Eighth Street takes advantage of the soaring
retail fenestration of the old Lansburgh department store.*

FERBANK MUSEUM OF NATURAL HISTORY

ATLANTA, GEORGIA

This museum is located along a lush residential parkway laid out early in the century by landscape architect Frederick Law Olmsted. At the rear of the site is a 65-acre original-growth hardwood preserve known as the Fernbank Forest. The new building reconciles this mixed landscape of lawn and woodlands by working from the former to establish a formal, public face for the museum, while harnessing the latter as a physical and symbolic link to Georgia's natural history.

Approached by a long processional drive, the building is set back from the street to reduce its apparent size in relation to its residential neighbors. Its flat and colonnaded two-story entry facade and distinctive cornice establish a strong civic character for the building and impart a sense of stateliness. At the rear of the site, where the topography slopes and the building meets the forest, the facade opens to nature with a three-story elevation whose organic, irregular pattern of fenestration and detailing differs dramatically from the symmetry of the building's front.

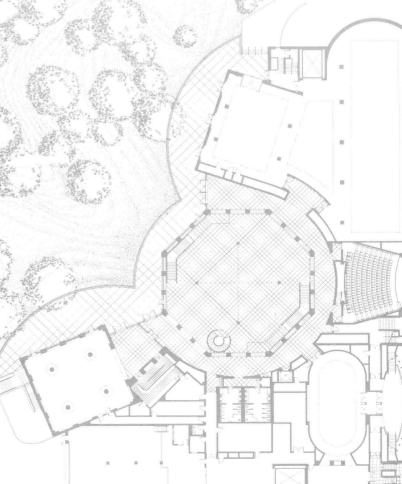

LOWER LEVEL

Internally, the building expresses its role as a natural history museum, addressing both nature itself and man's relationship to nature throughout history. Architectural references recall earlier civilizations as well as the early natural history museum as a building genre. Egyptian-inspired columns parade along the curved interior wall of the main entry hall, while a typographic frieze inscribed with the native American names for the rivers and islands of Georgia celebrates man's tradition of giving names to places and natural features. Architectural inscriptions and pictorials—lost architectural traditions —are revived in the natural history hall, which features a wrapping frieze-mural with cutout pictorial images of plants, animals, birds, and marine life.

At the heart of the museum is an enormous three-story light court—the great hall—whose soaring treelike columns make subtle reference to the space as a classical courtyard ruin. This space is conceived in deliberate contrast to the cloistered interiors of more traditional museums. Here the core is cut open to meet the landscape, symbolically connecting the inner world of the museum with the outer world of community and reflecting the museum's contemporary mission as a community-centered teaching institution.

As the building's main point of orientation, the great hall is an animated space that allows the circulation of people to all parts of the museum by means of cantilevered stairways, which wind and climb through the three-story volume. Its windows embrace the Fernbank Forest as an integral part of the museum's exhibitions, and flood the building's core with light and views.

The irregular form of the rear facade responds to the primitive character of the forest preserve it faces. The large windows of the great hall, at the center of this facade, give that space a transparency that allows man-made and natural environments to meet.

The main entry at Fernbank is defined by a grand arch flanked by spheres representing the earth and heavens. Freestanding columns enhance the civic presence of this formal facade.

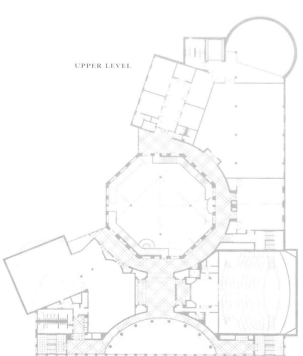

UPPER LEVEL

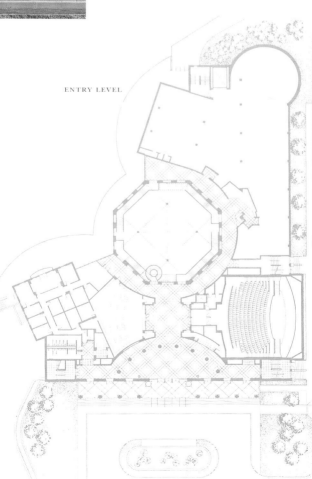

ENTRY LEVEL

The plans show high activity areas at the center ringed by specialized spaces—an IMAX theater and auditorium, permanent and traveling exhibit space, educational facilities, a restaurant, and a museum shop.

Inside the entry arch, the main lobby directs visitors through Fernbank's natural history hall to the great hall.

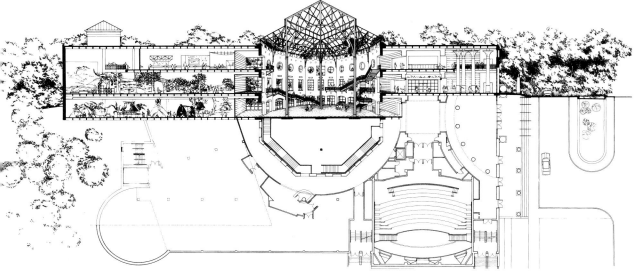

As the building's point of orientation and main gathering place, the great hall is an animated space with all the excitement and activity of an archaeological excavation site. The great hall completes the connection between the museum's inward focus and its view of the landscape.

DAVIDSON COLLEGE

DAVIDSON, NORTH CAROLINA

With its simple temple form, red brick skin, and expansive roof, Davidson's new visual arts building is firmly rooted in the college's tradition of strong, strictly ordered neo-classical architecture. Second-story porticoes on each of the gabled ends make a direct reference to the college's revered Debating Halls, while the side elevations make historical, though not literal, gestures in echoing the rhythmic structure and detailing of classical architecture.

Inside, the plan is organized with a simple ordering of program elements. Public spaces, including a lecture hall and art gallery, are clustered near the main entrance. Beyond the public spaces, the building becomes a factory for the making of art. Its imagery, scale, and proportions strike a balance between classical and industrial languages. The first-floor perimeter walls are lined with large, open studios for etching, lithography, and sculpture and with faculty offices. Individual painting studios line the second-story arcade; each is washed with natural light from the oversized arcade windows.

At the core of the building is an interior court-yard, which serves as a gathering space for students and a place for art exhibitions. It is also the primary orienta-tion and circulation space within the building. Naturally lit by a glazed skylight supported by lacy steel trusswork, the courtyard is an active, communal space. A punctuated, second-story interior "arcade" of doorways reflects the perimeter arcade of windows on the exterior wall. The vast space, making reference to the great basilicas of the classical era, connotes a community of artists and con-trasts with the building's heavily rooted and disciplined exterior expression.

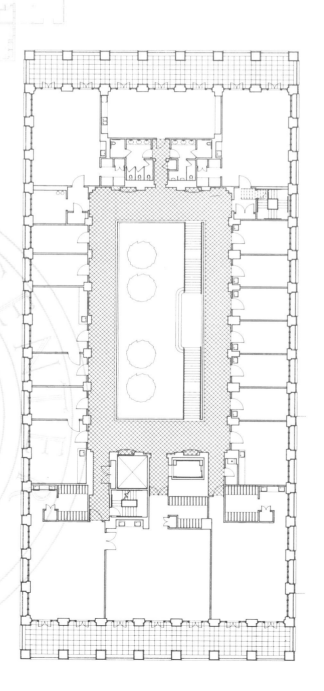

The building is entered below the templelike frontispiece into the court. A minor cross axis allows entry from the parking lot and terrace and separates the exhibit spaces from the main body of the building.

The two-and-a-half story west facade of the building is situated at the primary entrance to the campus and creates a strong first impression for visitors to the college. The somewhat smaller east facade faces the interior of the campus and Main Street. Its curved entry benches reach out to the students and community and invite them into the Visual Arts Center.

Throughout the grounds of St. Paul's School, a harmony exists between a rich variety of building types and landscape experiences. This thirty-student residence and its three faculty houses reflect this fluid relationship between building and landscape, which embodies the founding educational ideas of St. Paul's. Nature is presented as a source of empirical understanding, physical satisfaction, and spiritual enlightenment. A dynamic balance is achieved between multiple centers within the campus.

The faculty houses were designed as individual buildings to create a residential village centered around a courtyard garden. The arrangement is a microcosm of the larger campus idea.

In the student residence hall a single-loaded corridor opens the interior space to the garden and provides all students with a connection to the center of the residential community. A double-height common room is accessible from all areas of the student residence and provides the interior equivalent of the exterior garden space. Separate spaces for each student can be combined to create suites, allowing maximum flexibility of use. On the lower floors side-by-side student rooms can be used as living room and double bedroom, while on the upper floors vertically stacked student rooms provide for the creation of living room and sleeping loft. These combinations of space are reflected in the positioning of windows across the building's facades.

ST. PAUL'S SCHOOL   KEHAYA HOUSE

CONCORD, NEW HAMPSHIRE

NORTH ELEVATION

The eave lines vary between the student residence and the individual faculty houses, breaking down the overall mass of the building as it meets the surrounding landscape, following a tradition of country houses with smaller-scaled attached pavilions. Dormers and bays animate and further reduce the scale of the individual buildings, creating variety within a single vocabulary.

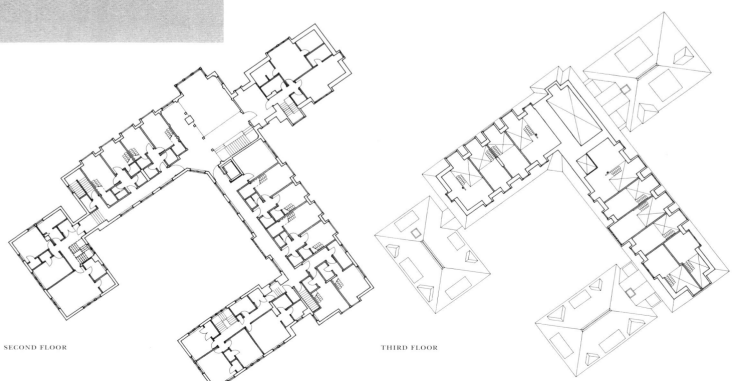

SECOND FLOOR

THIRD FLOOR

HARRISON OPERA HOUSE

NORFOLK, VIRGINIA

A hulking public works-built auditorium with cramped and dimly lit lobbies, Norfolk's former Center Theatre served as a venue for USO shows during World War II. Located in the city's cultural arts district near the Chrysler Art Museum, the building has been transformed into a contemporary 1,700-seat professional theater and opera hall.

Since one of the existing building's major flaws was its lack of appropriate gathering space, a new entry sequence was conceived, beginning with a dramatic new facade punctuated by four corner towers. The new construction surrounds the existing circa 1942 building on three sides, creating spaces within for new lobbies and support functions.

A new entrance vestibule provides connections to a lower level lobby as well as to two ceremonial spiral stairs, which wind through the front towers to the theater's Grand Lobby on the second level. One of the stairs continues its spiral upward to a third level gallery that overlooks the Grand Lobby and connects to the upper balconies of the theater's house. All of the spaces open to each other through multiple levels, allowing for lively interaction of opera patrons in the movement of the crowd and bringing the drama of the stage to the lobby.

Inside the all-new interior, two new levels of side boxes animate the walls of the house with people and bring the visual line of the seating down to the stage in the tradition of the great opera houses of Europe. The coffered ceiling is designed in a radial pattern that emphasizes the curve of the seating and balcony front.

The four exterior towers separate the mass of the theater from the fly loft behind and help to reestablish the building as an important element in the civic and cultural life of Norfolk. The towers are visible from all directions on a site that is exposed to the major roads around it. The new additions on the front and sides are glazed with tremendous overscaled windows, which reveal the excitement of the theater-going experience within.

The new two-story centerpiece Grand Lobby offers views of the Chrysler Museum and the Norfolk skyline while providing direct access to the balcony level of the theater and to new box seating. Off to each side, grand sweeping stairs in each tower lead to the lower lobby.

WILLIAM H. LINCOLN SCHOOL

BROOKLINE, MASSACHUSETTS

Reflecting a child's vision of the world, this new public elementary school marries function with fantasy. Located in a historic residential neighborhood, the building meanders across the site, an organic form articulated with an architectural villagescape composed of a rhythmic series of bays and simple gable elements. The variety of dormers that dot the roof enhances the reading of this metaphor and creates an appropriately childlike scale and character.

Inside, three classroom wings fan out from a main "street," which connects the more public spaces, including the library, cafeteria, gymnasium, and auditorium. Short corridors, like village "streets," connect a sequence of spaces that support and encourage interaction, exploration, and activity. Dormers, bays, and varied windows define multiple areas for learning within each classroom. Clusters of classrooms for each grade share a common activity and alternative learning space off the corridor.

On the second and third floors, the large roof forms create warm, inviting, atticlike spaces for classrooms, playing on the fantasy and sense of adventure and discovery associated with lost attic treasures.

The spatial variety and village atmosphere in the school create a unified whole out of a collection of parts, fostering a sense of community and promoting excitement about learning.

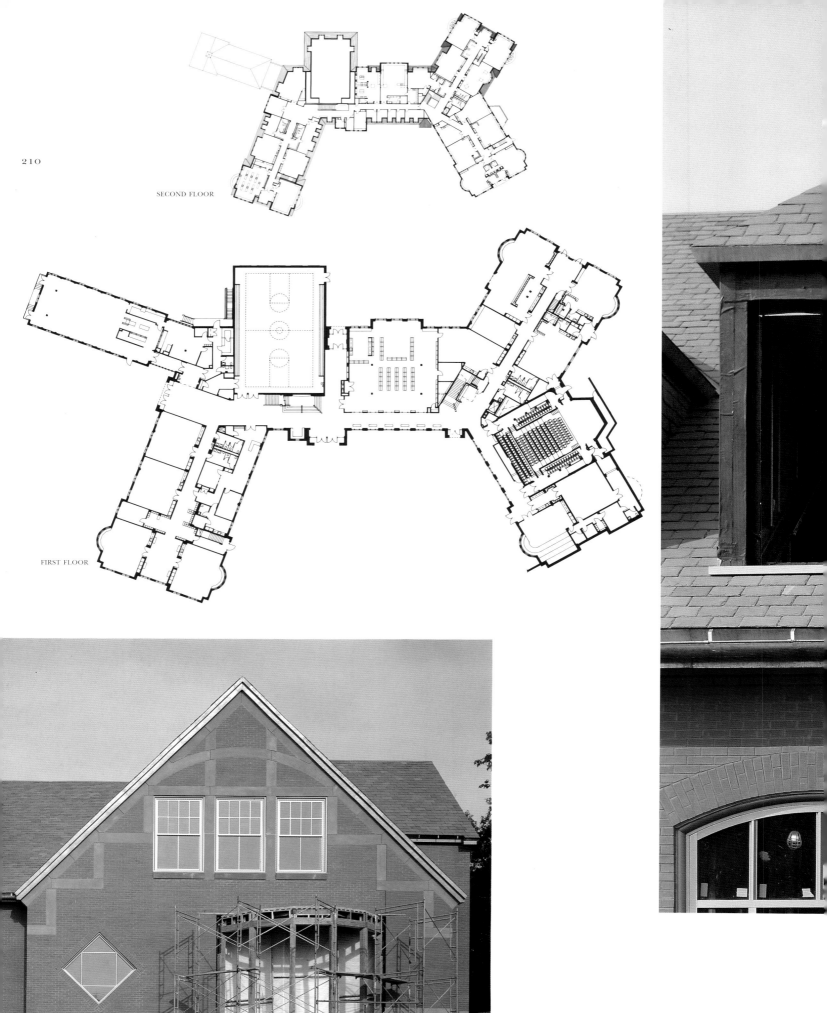

SECOND FLOOR

210

FIRST FLOOR

Detailed stonework creates a richness of texture and pattern in keeping with the surrounding historic Brookline neighborhood. To create a more intimate environment, the school is broken down into several wings, each housing classrooms for a separate age group.

D I S N E Y   V A C A T I O N   C L U B

INDIAN RIVER COUNTY, FLORIDA

This resort development draws upon the imagery and folklore of the Florida coastal resort towns that evolved in the years following the Civil War. Up and down the southern Atlantic coast, towns sprouted up around the lavish hotels founded by Henry Flagler, Henry Plant, and other entrepreneurs as they pushed the train route further and further south to satisfy the desires of a growing leisure class for places to winter.

The project, located on seventy acres of land along Florida's treasure coast, is conceived as a small town, a city in microcosm. The 115-room beachfront main building is the focal point and the gateway to the community, much as the old hotels served as gateways to southern Florida for travelers from the North. The design incorporates a rich variety of building scales, public activities, and circulation to create a living city.

The master plan is informal and pedestrian focused; automobiles are held to the perimeter streets. People move through natural areas to meandering pedestrian promenades along the lake or the ocean. The buildings are sited to explore the rich and varied ways in which man has historically inhabited the landscape. The formal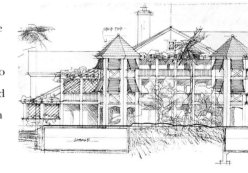

grand scale of the main building, the cluster of three oceanfront buildings around a courtyard, and the smaller-scaled beach and lakeside housing reflect the natural evolution of a grand resort town.

The architectural vocabulary uses the Shingle Style and the Stick Style as expressions of informal living in the landscape. The building masses vary from the simple, which sit on piers in the land, to the more fluid and complex, which grow organically out of the ground with roofscapes that read as landscapes.

The 16-unit Oceanfront Villas are broken down into three individual buildings grouped around a courtyard to create a residential scale. A variety of porches and balconies provide multiple view and scaling elements. One-story roof eaves with dormered upper floors further reinforce the residential scale.

GRAHAM GUND, born in 1940 in Cleveland, Ohio, was educated at Kenyon College and pursued postgraduate studies at the Rhode Island School of Design prior to enrolling in Harvard University's Graduate School of Design. While at Harvard he received two Master's degrees: one in Architecture (1968), and the other in Urban Design (1969).

Early in his professional career, Graham worked under Walter Gropius at The Architects Collaborative, and in 1971 established his own professional practice in Cambridge. He was joined by principals Peter Madsen, FAIA (1972-present), and David Perry, AIA (1974-1992). The three launched the practice with a major project, the Hyatt Regency Cambridge (1972-1977), at the same time garnering the firm's first AIA Honor Award for the Institute of Contemporary Art (1976).

Graham is active in the art and architecture communities of Boston. He has served as a trustee of the Boston Museum of Fine Arts, of the Institute of Contemporary Art, of the Society for the Preservation of New England Antiquities, and as a member of the Massachusetts General Hospital. He has been a director of the Boston Society of Architects; an overseer of the Boston Symphony Orchestra; and the founder and former chairman of the Boston Foundation for Architecture. He has served as a member of the Advisory Committee on the Arts at Harvard and Radcliffe colleges and on the Committee to Visit the Harvard Art Museums. On a national level, he is a Fellow of the American Institute of Architects; a member of the AIA's National Committee on Design; a trustee of the National Building Committee and of the National Trust for Historic Preservation; and he has served on the Collections Committee of the National Gallery of Art.

He holds honorary degrees from Kenyon College; the Massachusetts College of Art; the University of Massachusetts, Amherst, and Wheaton College.

PETER E. MADSEN, a native of Boston, was born in 1945 and educated at Harvard College before receiving a Master of Architecture from the Harvard University Graduate School of Design. He has served on the GSD's Alumni Council and has been a frequent guest critic. Prior to joining Graham Gund Architects, Peter worked with John Andrews, Anderson, Baldwin on the design of George Gund Hall at the Harvard Graduate School of Design.

Peter has been managing principal of GGA since joining the firm in 1972. He is a Fellow of the American Institute of Architects and an active member of the Boston Society of Architects, having served as a member of its board of directors. Outside of the office, he has focused on historic and landscape preservation work. He serves as vice president of the Trustees of Reservations, the largest private land trust in Massachusetts, and he is a trustee of the Society for the Preservation of New England Antiquities. He is a member of the Urban Land Institute and the Greater Boston Real Estate Board.

Peter and his wife Betsy are co-authors of *A Traveler's Guide to India* (Scribners, 1973).

THE SCHOOL-HOUSE
Housing First Honor Award, American Institute of Architects
Record Interiors, *Architectural Record*
Housing Award, Boston Society of Architects
Excellence in Architecture Award,
  New England Regional Council/AIA
Design Excellence in Housing Award,
  Boston Society of Architects

INSTITUTE OF CONTEMPORARY ART
Honor Award for Excellence in Design,
  American Institute of Architects

CARROLL CENTER FOR THE BLIND
Excellence in Architecture Award,
  New England Regional Council/AIA

SHAPLEIGH SUMMER RESIDENCE
Housing Award of Merit, American Institute of Architects
Housing Award, Boston Society of Architects
Excellence in Architecture Award,
  New England Regional Council/AIA
Record Houses, *Architectural Record*

DEUTSCH RESIDENCE
Record Houses, *Architectural Record*
Excellence in Architecture Award,
  New England Regional Council/AIA

CHURCH COURT
Honor Award for Excellence in Design,
  American Institute of Architects
Housing Award, Boston Society of Architects
Project of the Year, Builder's Choice , *Builder*
Harleston Parker Medal (Best Building of the Year),
  Boston Society of Architects
Best New Addition to the Skyline, *Boston Magazine*
Excellence in Architecture Award,
  New England Regional Council/AIA
Best Designs of the Year, *Time Magazine*
Design Citation, *Progressive Architecture*

BULFINCH SQUARE
Excellence in Architecture Award,
  New England Regional Council/AIA
Award for Conservation,
  Victorian Society New England Chapter
Grand Award, Builder's Choice, *Builder*

PATTERSON RESIDENCE
Record Houses, *Architectural Record*
Exports Award, Boston Society of Architects

NESBEDA RESIDENCE
Merit Award, Builder's Choice, *Builder*

THE SCHOOL-HOUSE ON MONUMENT SQUARE
Merit Award, Builder's Choice, *Builder*

COHEN RESIDENCE
Interior Architecture Design Award,
  Boston Society of Architects

ONE FANEUIL HALL SQUARE
Project Excellence Award,
  National Association of Industrial and Office Parks

CONNECTICUT COLLEGE
HORIZON ADMISSIONS BUILDING
Citation, *American School & University*

LINCOLN LIBRARY
Excellence in Architecture Award,
  New England Regional Council/AIA
Exports Award, Boston Society of Architects

75 STATE STREET
Project Excellence Award,
  National Association of Industrial and Office Parks
Tucker Architectural Award, Building Stone Institute

WATERVILLE VALLEY TOWN SQUARE
Exports Award, Boston Society of Architects

WESTMINSTER SCHOOL
CENTENNIAL PERFORMING ARTS CENTER
Award of Excellence, National Commercial Builders Council

NORTHEASTERN UNIVERSITY
HENDERSON BOATHOUSE
Excellence in Architecture Award,
  New England Regional Council/AIA
Citation, *American School & University*
Award for Conservation,
  Victorian Society New England Chapter

BOSTON BALLET
Award of Excellence, National Commercial
  Builders Council

THE LANSBURGH
Merit Award, Builder's Choice, *Builder*

HYATT REGENCY CAMBRIDGE
Environmental Improvement Award,
  Associated Landscape Contractors of America
Interior Design Award, *Institutions Magazine*
Outstanding Design Award, Massachusetts Masonry Institute

CONNECTICUT COLLEGE
BLAUSTEIN CENTER FOR THE HUMANITIES
Citation, *American School & University*
Exports Award, Boston Society of Architects

SCHOOL OF THE MUSEUM OF FINE ARTS
First Award/Design, International Masonry Institute

1973
Private Residence, Aspen, Colorado
Rockefeller Residence, Cambridge, Massachusetts

1974
Coppermine Farm Barn, Guest House, Griggstown, New Jersey

1975
Massachusetts Association for Blind, Life Learning Center, Project
  Boston, Massachusetts

1976
Hyatt Regency Cambridge Hotel, Cambridge, Massachusetts
Institute of Contemporary Art, Boston, Massachusetts

1977
Waterfront Hotel, Project, Boston, Massachusetts

1978
Shapleigh Summer Residence, Mishaum Point, Massachusetts
Webster Spring Company, Project, Oxford, Massachusetts
Willard Place/Dunfey Hotels, Project, Washington, D.C.

1979
The School-House Condominiums, Boston, Massachusetts
Old Port Hotel, Project, Portland, Maine

1980
Harvard University Squash Courts, Feasibility Study
  Cambridge, Massachusetts
Sargent's Wharf, Project, Boston, Massachusetts
Wentworth-By-The-Sea, Project, Portsmouth, New Hampshire

1981
Boston Society of Architects, The Architectural Bookstore
  Boston, Massachusetts
City of Boston School Reuse Survey, Boston, Massachusetts
Bowditch Park, Project, Salem, Massachusetts

1982
Synectics, Offices, Cambridge, Massachusetts
Engelhard Residence, Project, Cambridge, Massachusetts
Creek Square, Project, Boston, Massachusetts

1983
Church Court, Boston, Massachusetts
Deutsch Residence, Boston, Massachusetts
Davis Residence, South Dartmouth, Massachusetts
Patterson Residence, Fisher's Island, New York
Harvard University, Johnston Gatehouse
  Cambridge, Massachusetts
Allegheny County Jail & Courthouse, Feasibility Study
  Pittsburgh, Pennsylvania

1984
Bulfinch Square, Cambridge, Massachusetts
Carroll Center for the Blind, Newton, Massachusetts
Hyatt Regency Cambridge Hotel, Health Club
  Cambridge, Massachusetts
South End, Master Plan, Boston, Massachusetts
Stone Zoo, Master Plan, Stoneham, Massachusetts
Zero Arrow Street, Project, Cambridge, Massachusetts
Earthwatch, Project, Boston, Massachusetts
95 Berkeley Street, Project, Cambridge, Massachusetts
Frontage Road Office Building, Project
  Boston, Massachusetts

1985
Arnot Art Museum, Elmira, New York
678 Massachusetts Avenue, Cambridge, Massachusetts
Riverwalk Hotel, Project, Lawrence, Massachusetts
First National Bank of Ipswich, Project
  Ipswich, Massachusetts

1986
Connecticut College, Blaustein Center for the Humanities
  New London, Connecticut
Cohen Residence, Boston, Massachusetts
Nesbeda Residence, Harvard, Massachusetts
Fuller Block, Boston, Massachusetts
Radcliffe College, Bunting Institute, Cambridge, Massachusetts
90 Canal Street, Boston, Massachusetts
Osterville Town Center, Feasibility Study
  Osterville, Massachusetts
Boston Center for Arts, Master Plan, Boston, Massachusetts
161 First Street, Cambridge, Massachusetts
Cone Communications Offices, Boston, Massachusetts
Newharbor, Master Plan, Providence, Rhode Island
25 Huntington Avenue, Project, Boston, Massachusetts
Lowell Mills, Project, Lowell, Massachusetts

1987
9-11 Mt. Auburn Street, Cambridge, Massachusetts
Plimoth Plantation Visitors Center, Plymouth, Massachusetts
School of the Museum of Fine Arts, Boston, Massachusetts
The School-House on Monument Square
  Charlestown, Massachusetts
Battery Wharf, Project, Boston, Massachusetts

1988
Maritime Center at Norwalk, Norwalk, Connecticut
One Faneuil Hall Square, Boston, Massachusetts
600 Memorial Drive, Cambridge, Massachusetts
Congress Street Pedestrian Overpass, Feasibility Study
  Boston, Massachusetts
Merchants Row, Boston, Massachusetts
Clarendon Square, Project, Boston, Massachusetts

1989
Waterville Valley Town Square, Waterville Valley, New Hampshire
Golden Eagle Lodge, Waterville Valley, New Hampshire
75 State Street, Boston, Massachusetts,
  with Skidmore, Owings, and Merrill, Architect & Engineers
Lincoln Library, Lincoln, Massachusetts
Westminster School, Centennial Performing Arts Center
  Simsbury, Connecticut
Connecticut College, Horizon Admissions Building
  New London, Connecticut
Shapleigh Residence, Ladue, Missouri
Northeastern University, Henderson Boathouse
  Boston, Massachusetts
One Bowdoin Square, Boston, Massachusetts
Cardinal Cushing Park, Boston, Massachusetts
Spiro Residence, Edgartown, Massachusetts
Massachusetts General Hospital, Alzheimer's Disease Care Center,
  Feasibility Study, Boston, Massachusetts
Dalton Street Housing, Project, Boston, Massachusetts
Lewis Wharf, Project, Boston, Massachusetts

1990
University of New Hampshire, Library, Feasibility Study
  Durham, New Hampshire
American University, Performing Arts Center, Project
  Washington, D.C.
Society for the Preservation of New England Antiquities,
  Conservation Center, Project, Waltham, Massachusetts
Massachusetts General Hospital, Master Plan & Feasibility Study
  Boston, Massachusetts
The Channing House, Project, Cambridge, Massachusetts
Museum of American Textile History, Project
  Lawrence, Massachusetts

1991
Concord Museum, Concord, Massachusetts
The Village Commons, South Hadley, Massachusetts
The Lansburgh, Washington, D.C.
Boston Ballet, Boston, Massachusetts
Mt. Holyoke College, Williston Library, South Hadley, Massachusetts
The Inn at Harvard, Cambridge, Massachusetts
Rockefeller Residence Addition, Cambridge, Massachusetts
Inn at Kennebunkport, Feasibility Study, Kennebunkport, Maine

1992
Fernbank Museum of Natural History, Atlanta, Georgia
University of The South, Gailor Hall, Project, Sewanee, Tennessee
University of The South, Studio Arts Building, Project
  Sewanee, Tennessee
Concord Academy, Dormitory, Project, Concord, Massachusetts
The Ski Market, Feasibility Study, Brookline, Massachusetts
Westminster School, Cushing Hall, Master Plan, Simsbury, Connecticut
This Old House, Lexington, Massachusetts

1993
Davidson College, Visual Arts Center, Davidson, North Carolina
Enders Residence, Waterford, Connecticut
Museum of Cape Ann History, Gloucester, Massachusetts
The William H. Lincoln School, Brookline, Massachusetts
Harrison Opera House, Norfolk, Virginia,
  with Williams, Tazewell and Associates, Architect
St. Paul's School, Kehaya House, Concord, New Hampshire
Disney Inn, Celebration, Florida
Disney Vacation Club, Indian River County, Florida
Woods Hole Oceanographic Institute, Discovery Center, Feasibility
  Study, Woods Hole, Massachusetts

1994 (All projects are in progress)
Centre East Performing Arts Center, Skokie, Illinois
Disney Resort and Convention Center
  Lake Buena Vista, Florida
The Nantucket House, Nantucket, Massachusetts
The Lawrenceville School, Library, Lawrenceville
  New Jersey
Cape Cod Center for the Performing Arts, Master Plan
  Mashpee, Massachusetts
Rehabilitation Hospital of the Cape and Islands
  Sandwich, Massachusetts
Case Western Reserve University, Law School, Cleveland, Ohio
The Lawrenceville School, Music Building
  Lawrenceville, New Jersey
Franklin Park Zoo, Predator/Prey Exhibit
  Boston, Massachusetts
Cheekwood Museum and Botanical Gardens
  Nashville, Tennessee

220

1975

Kay, J. H. "New Art Takes Off from Worn-angle Frame." *Boston Globe*, September 7, 1975.

Neely, A. "At Last, the ICA Has Come Home." *The Patriot Ledger* (Boston), May 6, 1975.

Rose, B. "Fantasy vs. Reality: The news is conceptual architecture, recycled buildings." *Vogue* (May 1975): 28.

Yudis, A. "Recycled Police Station a Haven for Art." *Boston Globe*, April 27, 1975.

1976

Campbell, R. "Stairway for the Starers." *Boston Sunday Globe*, April 11, 1976.

Blake, P. "Constabulary reconsecrated." *Progressive Architecture* (November 1976): 45.

"A permanent home for the Institute of Contemporary Art." *Interior Design* (December 1976): 148-51.

1977

"Hyatt Regency Cambridge, A New Shape for an Urban Hotel." *Architectural Record* (October 1977): 110-13.

1978

Morgan, J. "Hyatt Regency Cambridge." *Interiors* (November 1978): 76-79.

"Richardsonian Police Station Becomes a Gallery." *AIA Journal* (May 1978).

"Back to the Barn." *House & Garden* (July 1978): 106-9. (Coppermine Farm Barn)

"De-institutionalizing for the blind." *Progressive Architecture* (April 1978): 92-93.

"Hotel—Hyatt Regency, Cambridge, Massachusetts." *Baumeister* (December 1978): 1083.

"When Architects Pick America's Best Buildings." *US News and World Report* (July 17, 1978).

1979

Guralnick, E. "A Generational Hideaway." *Boston Sunday Globe Magazine*, August 5, 1979.

"Shapleigh Residence." *Nikkei Architecture* (1979): 5-12.

"Shapleigh house on the Massachusetts coast." *Architectural Record—Record Houses of 1979* (Mid-May 1979): 50-53.

"Shapleigh House." *The Toshi-Jutako* (October 1979): 5-12.

1980

Yudis, A. "Perkins school on St. Botolph gets new life." *Boston Sunday Globe*, April 27, 1980.

"Haus in Massachusetts." *Baumeister* (March 1980): 248-51.

"Shapleigh Residence, Massachusetts." *L'industria Delle Construzion* (Agosto 1980): 53-55.

"Vertical Space: A Service Wing Becomes a Home." *House and Garden* (May-June 1980): 160-63.

1981

Baltozer, D. "Graham Gund: quietly shaping the future." *Patriot Ledger* (Boston), September 22, 1981.

Campbell, R. "Postmodernism goes to school." *Boston Sunday Globe Magazine*, July 12, 1981.

Lewin, S. "An 1891 Schoolhouse Gears Up for 20th Century Living." *House Beautiful* (September 1981): 97-99.

"Schoolhouse condominiums." *Nikkei Architecture* (1981): 46-47.

"The Rise and Fall of a 19th Century Schoolhouse—Record Interiors 1981." *Architectural Record* (Mid-February 1981): 70-73.

"Graham Gund Associates: Church Condominiums." *Progressive Architecture* (January 1981): 154-55.

1982

Rabinowitz, B. "A New Training Center for the Blind." *The Magazine* (May 1982): 14-18.

"Classrooms for the blind occupy a renovated stable." *Architectural Record* (June 1982): 86-89.

"Attic Remodeled to a Living Space." *Housing* (January 1982): 101.

"Remodeled School Building—Cambridge, Massachusetts." *Housing* (August 1982): 51.

1983

"A schoolhouse converted." *House Beautiful's Home Remodeling* (Spring 1983): 56-59.

"Townhouse renovation, Boston, Massachusetts." *Architectural Record—Record Houses of 1983* (May 1983): 134-37. (Deutsch residence)

"Deutsch House." *The Toshi-Jutaku* (November 1983): 43-46.

1984

Campbell, R. "Church Court—a bright new face on the Boston riverscape." *Boston Globe*, March 4, 1984.

Craig, L. "Alternative Space—Graham Gund." *Art New England* (March 1984): 8-9.

King, J. "Neighborhood Shaker." *The Patriot Ledger* (Boston) October 24, 1984.

Muro, M. "Converts: Former churches offer unique opportunities for architectural recycling." *Boston Globe*, June 1, 1984.

Vogel, C. "Hanging up a New Shingle." *New York Times Magazine*, April 8, 1984.

Von Eckardt, W. "Classic Values, New Forms." *Time*, January 2, 1984, 72-73.

Yudis, A. "A new life for the old Middlesex Courthouse." *Boston Globe*, March 4, 1984.

"Private House, Northeastern Coast." *Architectural Record* (Mid-April 1984): 84-87. (Patterson residence)

"Haus in Boston." *Baumeister* (July 1984): 40-42.

"Wohnen bei der Kirche in Boston." *Baumeister* (June 1984): 61-63.

"Summer Residence." *Global Architecture Houses #15* (1984): 160-65.

1985

Boles, D. "Assessing a winner." *Progressive Architecture* (February 1985): 88-94.

Campbell, R. "Church Ruins Wall Condominiums." *Architecture* (May 1985): 256-61.

Campbell, R. "An original Post-Modernist" *Boston Sunday Globe Magazine*, December 1, 1985.

Fisher, T. "Graham Gund Associates—Architects as Developer." *Progressive Architecture* (July 1985): 105-10.

Murray, S. "A Change in Vacation Lifestyles." *Homes International* (September/October 1985): 7-13.

Temin, C. "The art and architecture of Graham Gund." *Boston Sunday Globe Magazine*, December 1, 1985.

"Architects Pick the Best of the New." *US News & World Report* July 1, 1985.

"Townhouse—New Building and Old Church." *Builder* (October 1985): 136-41.

"Enlivening the Shingle Style." *House Beautiful's Building Manual* (Fall/Winter 1985-86): 78-81.

1986

Campbell, R. "Stately Ensemble Unified by a Courtyard." *Architecture* (May 1986): 152-57.

Carlock, M. "A new home for the Museum School." *Boston Sunday Globe*, August 3, 1986.

Leventhal, E. "How Historic Structures and Modern Needs Can Be Reconciled." *Construction Products Review* (September 1986): 50-53.

Stange, E. "Brave New Boston." *Boston Herald*, February 16, 1986.

Vogel, C. "A Sense of Place." *New York Times Magazine*, PART 2, April 13, 1986.

Vogel, C. "Summer House by the Sea." *New York Times Magazine*, PART 2, April 13, 1986.

"Grand Award—Bulfinch Square." *Builder* (October 1986): 158-59.

"Apartment Building—Church Court." *Architectural Record* (June 1986): 97.

1987

Campbell, R. "New visitor center upstages Plantation." *Boston Globe,* November 24, 1987.

Cormier, L. "Choreography of Space: Graham Gund's Museum School Complex." *Art New England* (February 1987): 13.

Salisbury, W. "The soaring imagination of a native son." *The Plain Dealer Magazine* (Cleveland) January 11, 1987.

"Charlestown High School Apartments." *Builder* (October 1987): 172-73.

"The School of the Museum of Fine Arts Addition and Renovation— Boston, Massachusetts." *AS&U* (November 1987): 180.

"Apartment Building—Remodeled Department Store." *Progressive Architecture* (August 1987): 27.

"Roof with a View." *Home* (June 1987): 38-41.

1988

Baumann, P. "First impressions are important." *The Day* (New London, Conn.) March 22, 1988.

Campbell, R. "Graham Gund, A Massachusetts Residence Inspired by Stables." *Architectural Digest* (August 1988): 60-65.

Campbell, R. "Architecture: Graham Gund." *Architectural Digest* (February 1988): 128-33. (Cohen residence)

Forgey, B. "Graham Gund's Brave New Buildings." *Washington Post* January 9, 1988.

Pantridge, M. "Gund's World." *Boston Magazine,* November 1988.

Radin, C. "A center grows in South Hadley." *Boston Globe,* November 22, 1988.

Von Eckardt, W. "Friends, Lovers, and Families." *Washingtonian* (April 1988): 76.

"Graham Gund - Residence Award." *Builder* (October 1988): 168-69.

"Office Building." *Progressive Architecture* (February 1988): 40.

1989

Campbell, R. "A cheer for 75 State Street—a winner, warts and all." *Boston Sunday Globe,* April 23, 1989.

Campbell, R. "Gund's library has storybook charm." *Boston Globe,* August 1989.

Campbell, R. "Building on the pleasure principal." *Boston Sunday Globe,* December 1989.

Campbell, R. "Glittering & Controversial" *Architecture* (December 1989): 76-79.

Goldberger, P. "Proof That All That Glitters Is Not Vulgar." *New York Times,* August 13, 1989.

Goodspeed, L. "One Bowdoin Square: New Look for Historic Location." *s/f* (July/August 1989): 25-26.

Pitoniak, E. "A Touch of New England Class." *Ski* (December 1989): 1E-6E.

Tree, C. "Waterville Valley builds a village to remember." *Boston Globe,* February 5, 1989.

"Boston Architecture—Graham Gund Architects." *a & u* (April 1989): 87-90.

"Connecticut College Admissions Building." *AS&U—Architectural Portfolio* (November 1989): 49.

"Davidson College Gallery, Art History and Student Arts Facility." *AS&U—Architectural Portfolio* (November 1989).

"Small-town Village." *Architectural Record* (September 1989):102-3.

1990

Campbell, R. "Architectural promises that go unfulfilled." *Boston Globe,* July 24, 1990.

Campbell, R. "Lincoln Library Wins 'Export Award'." *Boston Globe,* May 8, 1990.

Goldberger, P. "After Opulence, a New 'Lite' Architecture." *New York Times,* May 20, 1990.

Howley, K. "Oasis springs from the ashes." *Boston Herald,* June 29, 1990.

"Team Spirit—Northeastern University Boathouse." *Architecture* (August 1990): 72-75.

"Town and Country." *Architectural Record* (February 1990): 128-31.

"Theatrical Romance." *Architectural Record* (August 1990): 83, 90-91.

"Clothing Store Building." *Architecture* (December 1990): 70-71.

"Office Building." *Architecture* (July 1990): 91-93.

"Northeastern University, Henderson Boathouse." *AS&U* (November 1990): 48.

"Westminster School, Centennial Performing Arts Center." *AS&U—Architectural Portfolio* (November 1990): 267.

1991

Campbell, R. "Gund's Ballet building is a light delight." *Boston Globe,* July 1991.

Campbell, R. "Concord museum minds its manners too well." *Boston Globe,* October 4, 1991.

Campbell, R. "Harvard Inn has left no room for daring." *Boston Globe,* December 13, 1991.

Chaison, N. "Now for Some Good News: Education Update." *s/f* (March/April 1991).

Clements, J. "Harvard keeping in character with new hotel." *Boston Globe,* August 5, 1991.

Cohen, R. "Two museums: Only one works." *Boston Herald,* April 28, 1991.

Diesenhouse, S. "A High-Tech Ballet Center in Boston." *New York Times,* August 4, 1991.

Fanger, I. "Boston Ballet dances for joy in airy new South End Home." *Sunday Boston Herald,* July 7 , 1991.

Gambon, J. "Designing a museum." *Boston Business Journal,* April 29, 1991.

Kay, J.H. "Terms of Endearment." *Architectural Digest* (August 1991): 118-23.

Taylor, R. "Concord's fresh eye on the past" *Boston Globe,* September 21, 1991.

Van Tuyl, L. "A Building Created with Ballet in Mind." *Christian Science Monitor,* July 30, 1991.

Wilson, S. "State Street." *Boston Globe,* January 3, 1991.

1992

Erstein, H. "Scene changes for Shakespeare cast." *Washington Times,* (Washington, D.C.), July 30, 1991.

Forgey, B. "Savory Stew— The Lansburgh Building, Mixing It Up." *Washington Post,* February 22, 1992.

Fox, C. "Museum melds best of old, new." *Atlanta Journal/ Atlanta Constitution,* October 4, 1992.

Gamerman, A. "The High-Tech Approach to the World Around Us." *Wall Street Journal,* October 27, 1992.

Richards, D. "Much Ado About Shakespeare in Washington." *New York Times,* March 15, 1992.

Seabrook, C. "At Fernbank, getting it right is all important." *Atlanta Journal/Atlanta Constitution,* October 3, 1992.

Thiele, J. "By the Yard." *Contract Design* (December 1992): 39-41.

"Capital Gains." *Architecture* (April 1992): 74-79.

"Bracing History." *Architecture* (April 1992): 85-89.

1993

Campbell, R. "Fernbank: Life tamed into entertainment." *Boston Globe,* February 19, 1993.

"Spanning Time." *Architectural Record* (January 1993): 74-81.

"Fernbank Museum of Natural History." *Architectural Record* (May 1993): 80-87.

Wells, J. "On a Human Scale." *The Patriot Ledger* (Boston) 1993.

"Institute of Contemporary Art." *Boston Arts.* 376-78.

PRINCIPALS
Graham Gund
Peter E. Madsen
David T. Perry

SENIOR ASSOCIATES
Richard Bechtel
William Erickson
Youngmin Jahan

ASSOCIATES
Leonard J. Bertaux
Elizabeth Redman
  Bramhall
Laura Sanden Cabo
Nelson K. Chen
George Coon
James Cullion
Jonilla Dorsten
Gerard Frank
Alec Holser
Mary Horst
L. Franklyn Lucas
James McComas
John Prokos
Don Self
Emily Sprague
Ann Voda
Lowell Warren, III
Gary Wolf
Willie Wayne Wong

LEFT TO RIGHT
Front: Jonilla Dorsten, Peter Madsen.
Middle: Elizabeth Redman Bramhall, Laura Sanden Cabo, Youngmin Jahan, Mary Horst, Alec Holser, James Cullion.
Back: John Prokos, George Coon

STAFF LIST

STAFF

Luann Abrahams
Alahe Aldo
Evelyn Alexandre
Blake Allison
Anthony Anderson
Ingrid Anderson
Robert Arthur
Jennifer Baker
Sandra Baptie
Derek Barcinski
Katharine Barrows
Julia Shaw-Bartels
John Bates
Marianne Beagan
Russ Beaudin
Carl Beers
Donald Beeson
Lynn Belinsky
Richard Bernstein
Rodrigo Bilbao
Marlon Blackwell
Heather Blair
Judith Bowen
Constantin Boym
Lance T. Braht
Robert Bramhall
Roland Brito
Lisa Brochu
Donalda Buchanan
Robert Buckham
Cathy Busch
Heather Campbell
Susan Cannon
Donna Carrier
Thomas Catalano
Miltos Catomeris
Sheilah Cavanaugh
Christopher Chan
Frank Chang
Donna Church
Christopher Clark
Mary Clifford
Katherine Cochran
Vincent Codispoti
Alexander E. Colt
Marc Cornett
Kathyanne Cowles
William Crozier
Stephen Dadagian
Stephanie A. Davis
Pompey Delafield
Kathy Delgreco
Michael Dembowski
Paul Demosthenes
Martin Dermady
Sarah Dewey
Katherine Dillon
Susan Doherty
Randy Doi
Maria Fernandez
   Donovan

Peter Dubin
Frank Edwards
David Eisen
Amy Eliot
Carl Erikson
Karen Fairbanks
John Felix
Catherine Fernandez
Joseph Ferrara
Albert Filoni
Dennis Findley
Beth Firkins
Michael Firkins
Donald Flaggs
Paul Frazier
Katherine Freygang
Tobias Gabranski
Donna Gadbois
Joanne Gaines
Evelyn Garber
Christine Garrett
Amy Gendler
Mira Gess
Donald Gheen
James Gleason
Eric Gould
Ramsay Gourd
Duncan Grant
Sarah Graves
Noah Grunberg
Mark Haber
Barbara Halford
Ellen Harkins
Jane Harrington
Lisa Healy
Robert Heineman
Lizbeth Herbert
Angela Herron
Vernon Herzeelle
Eric Hollenberg
Debbie Holmes
Lynn Hopkins
Arch Horst
Markus Hotz
Tony Hsiao
Carol Hsiung
Frances Chin-Jo Hsu
Christopher Insley
Susan Israel
Chris Iwerks
Gary Jereczek
Alexandra Johnston
Susan Berger Jones
Diane Kasprowicz
Mark Keiser
Edward Kelly
Kenneth Klos
Joan Koppel
Marsha Kulhonen
Margaret Lackner
Manuela LaCount
Christian Langmuir

Dongik Lee
Gloria Yim Lei Lim
Nancy Lippincott
Jay Litman
John Lodge
Kathleen Lugosch
Scott MacPherson
Carla Turner Macy
Tom Maloney
Eric Maltman
Douglas Manley
Ann Marshall
Emily Mather
Robert McCauley
Paula McGarry
Dee McKee
Jeffrey McLaughlin
Robin Meierding
Laura Miller
Julie Miner
Hitomi Mochidome
Kelly Monnahan
Elizabeth Morgan
Linda Morrison
Ping Mo
Judith Mulhern
Doris Nelson
Lisa Nelson
Sarah Newbury
Thomas Nohr
Charles Nutter
Eric Olsen
Ron Ostberg
John Ostlund
Mary Michael O'Hare
Kathleen O'Meara
Ann O'Rahilly
Richard Panciera
Thomas Parks
Mark Pederson
Dominic Pedulla
Michael Perera
Betty Pisano
Richard Potestio
John Powell
Donald Powers
Kevin Provencher
Timothy Quirk
Shirley Ransom
Bennett Reed
Ann Marie Reilly
Patrick Reynolds
Sylvia Richards
Mary Ann Rich
William Ridge
Dennis Rieske
Kenneth Roberts
John Ronan
Richard Rosa
Dan Rutledge
Elizabeth Saltonstall
Elena Saporta

Kim Schaefer
Graham Schelter
Jennifer Schelter
Kristin Schelter
Benjamin Schreier
Donna Schumacher
Garry Scoby
Mary Ann Sgarlat
William H. Sherman
Monica Sidor
Thaddeus Siemasko
Laura Silva
Daniel Simpson
Scott Slarsky
Edward J. Smith
Jessica Smith
Karen Spence
David Spinelli
James Spinelli
Barry Stanton
Sarah Stanton
Thomas Stark
Madeleine Steczynski
Rachel Steczynski
Barry Stedman
Clark Steven
Margaret Stier
Donna Stillway
Jonathan Strand
Raymond A. Streeter
Margot Street
Lena Sundgren
John Tadewald
Wendy Tardrew
Donald Taylor
Danah Tench
Denise Thompson
Lynne Thom
Michael Tingley
Eva Siu-Tracy
Pamela Trochesset
James Tsakirgis
Christine Verbitzki
Carl von Stetten
Phillip Wagner
Sharon Walcott
Tracy Walton
Mark Wamble
Michael Wang
George Warner
Elizabeth Wastler
Paul Weber
Andrew J. Weiser
Jackie Welsh
Andrew Wen
Kym Wheaton
Charles Willse
Jane Wilson
Peter Witmer
Jaya Kader Zebede
Gyorgy Zsilak

italics indicate former staff

INTRODUCTION
All photographs by Greg Heins, except page 10, Christo, *Running Fence, Sonoma and Marin Counties, California, 1972–76,* by Jeanne-Claude, and page 12 by Art Resource

THE SCHOOL-HOUSE
All photographs by Steve Rosenthal

THE INSTITUTE OF CONTEMPORARY ART
All photographs by Steve Rosenthal, except page 25 by Peter Jones

THE CARROLL CENTER FOR THE BLIND
All photographs by Steve Rosenthal

SHAPLEIGH SUMMER RESIDENCE
All photographs by Steve Rosenthal, except pages 32 lower and 33 courtesy of Graham Gund Architects

DEUTSCH RESIDENCE
All photographs by Steve Rosenthal

CHURCH COURT
All photographs by Steve Rosenthal, except pages 42, 45 upper and middle, and 48 upper courtesy of Graham Gund Architects

DAVIS RESIDENCE
All photographs by Steve Rosenthal

BULFINCH SQUARE
All photographs by Steve Rosenthal, except pages 57, 58 lower, and 60 upper courtesy of Graham Gund Architects, page 59 Gorchev and Gorchev, pages 62 lower and 63 by Willard Traub.

PATTERSON RESIDENCE
All photographs by Steve Rosenthal

NESBEDA RESIDENCE
All photographs by Steve Rosenthal, except page 71 by Alex S. MacLean/Landslides

THE SCHOOL-HOUSE ON MONUMENT SQUARE
All photographs by Steve Rosenthal

COHEN RESIDENCE
All photographs by Warren Jagger

PLIMOTH PLANTATION
All photographs by Steve Rosenthal, except page 91 by Lincoln Russell

ONE FANEUIL HALL SQUARE
All photographs by Steve Rosenthal, except page 99 by David Hewitt

CONNECTICUT COLLEGE ADMISSIONS
All photographs by Steve Rosenthal

LINCOLN LIBRARY
All photographs by Steve Rosenthal

ONE BOWDOIN SQUARE
All photographs by Warren Jagger

75 STATE STREET
All photographs by Steve Rosenthal, except page 115 upper by Warren Jagger

GOLDEN EAGLE LODGE
All photographs by David Hewitt, except page 118 upper by Nick Wheeler

WATERVILLE VALLEY TOWN CENTER
Photographs on pages 122 and 123 by David Hewitt, pages 124–127 by Nick Wheeler, except page 126 upper by David Hewitt

WESTMINSTER SCHOOL CENTENNIAL CENTER
All photographs by Steve Rosenthal

NORTHEASTERN BOATHOUSE
All photographs by Steve Rosenthal, except photographs on page 134 by Russ Sparkman/Northeastern University and page 137 by Alex S. MacLean/Landslides

SHAPLEIGH RESIDENCE
Photographs on pages 140, 142, and 143 upper by Alise O'Brien, pages 141, 143 lower, 144, 145 lower, 146 upper, and 147 by Tony Soluri, page 145 upper courtesy of Graham Gund Architects

THE INN AT HARVARD
All photographs by Warren Jagger, except page 147 by Steve Rosenthal

BOSTON BALLET
All photographs by Steve Rosenthal

THE VILLAGE COMMONS AT SOUTH HADLEY
Photographs on pages 160, 162, 163, 166 upper, and 167 by David Hewitt, pages 161 and 165 by Steve Rosenthal, pages 164 and 166 middle by Adam Laipson, page 164 lower by Elizabeth Gill Lui

MT. HOLYOKE LIBRARY
Photographs on pages 170 and 172 by Warren Jagger, pages 171, 174 upper, 175, and 176 by Adam Laipson, page 173 upper by Steve Rosenthal, page 173 lower by Clemens Kalischer

THE LANSBURGH
All photographs by Jeff Goldberg/Esto Photographics, except pages 180 upper and 181 courtesy of Graham Gund Architects, pages 182 and 183 upper by Carol Highsmith

FERNBANK MUSEUM
All photographs by Jonathan Hillyer

DAVIDSON COLLEGE
All photographs by Jonathan Hillyer

HARRISON OPERA HOUSE
All photographs by Bob Ander

WILLIAM H. LINCOLN SCHOOL
All photographs by David Desroches

PHOTOGRAPHERS' CREDITS

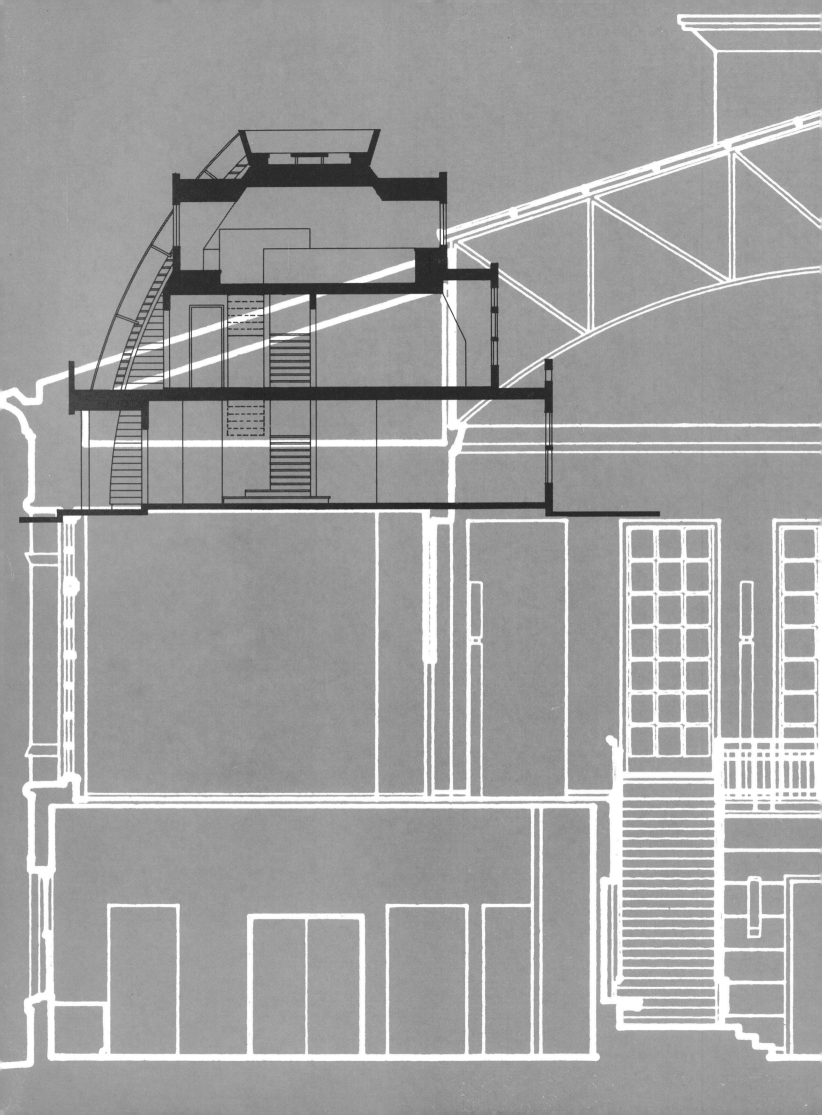